Not-so-humble
vegetables
from the Home Library Test Kitchen

Cole's Home Library Cookbooks
Glen Ellen, California

Not-so-humble vegetables

Contents

Chinese water spinach with crispy noodles, page 15

Bell pepper, garbanzo and olive salad; Roasted bell peppers with port and basil dressing, page 36

Beet skewers, page 31

Roman-style green beans, page 25

Veggies by any other name...
Some vegetable names may seem unusual, this is because vegetables may carry more than one common name. Depending on where you live, let the pictures adjacent to the recipes in this Cole's Home Library Cookbook be your guide to help you recognize and find what you are looking for at your local supermarket or green grocer.

For more Cole's Home Library information on Vegetables, including new cookbooks, see page 128 or come to Cole's web site, www.coleshomelibrary.com, for an interactive tour of what is happening in the world of cooking, gardening, and crafts for today's creative lifestyle.

Artichokes

An edible bud of a thistle-like member of the daisy family, the globe artichoke comes to us from North Africa. The Jerusalem artichoke, however, is neither from Jerusalem nor even an artichoke, but a crisp tuber tasting a bit like water chestnut and named after the Italian word for sunflower, girasole.

Globe artichokes

COOKING METHODS *Cooking times are based on 5 medium globe artichokes, bases trimmed to sit flat, tough outer leaves discarded, rinsed under cold water.*

*• **BOIL** Add artichokes to large pan of boiling water; boil, uncovered, about 30 minutes or until artichoke hearts are tender when pierced with a fork. Drain upside down; remove hairy choke with a spoon and discard it.*

*• **STEAM** Place artichokes in single layer in steamer basket; cook, covered, over pan of simmering water about 40 minutes or until tender. Drain upside down; remove hairy choke with a spoon and discard it.*

*• **MICROWAVE** Place artichokes and ¼ cup water in large microwave-safe dish. Cover, microwave on HIGH (100%) 15 minutes, pausing halfway during cooking time to turn. Drain upside down; remove hairy choke with a spoon and discard it.*

Tested in an 850-watt oven

OPPOSITE FROM TOP: Artichoke and Fava Bean Salad; Artichokes with Braised Prosciutto and Tomatoes

BRAISED ARTICHOKES WITH PROSCIUTTO AND TOMATOES

4 medium artichokes
3 tablespoons lemon juice
16 slices prosciutto
3 tablespoons olive oil
1 large onion, chopped
1½ tablespoons chopped fresh oregano
1½ tablespoons tomato paste
14oz can tomatoes, undrained, crushed
½ cup dry white wine
1 teaspoon chicken stock base or bouillon cube

Boil, steam or microwave artichokes until just tender; drain. Quarter artichokes, remove and discard choke; brush artichoke pieces with juice. Wrap 1 slice prosciutto around each artichoke piece, secure with toothpick.

Heat oil in large pan; cook artichoke bundles, in batches, until prosciutto is browned all over. Remove from pan; remove and discard toothpicks. Cook onion in same pan, stirring, until soft. Add remaining ingredients; simmer, covered, about 10 minutes or until sauce thickens slightly. Add artichokes; simmer, covered, about 10 minutes or until heated through and tender.

Serves 4 to 6.

■ Best made just before serving.
■ Freeze: Not suitable.

ARTICHOKE AND FAVA BEAN SALAD

4 medium artichokes
¼ cup lemon juice
½ cup olive oil
1 teaspoon sugar
1 clove garlic, crushed
⅓ cup chopped fresh mint
1lb packet frozen fava or lima beans, cooked
1⅓ cups kalamata olives

Boil, steam or microwave artichokes until just tender; drain. Quarter artichokes; remove and discard choke.

Combine juice, oil, sugar, garlic and mint in jar; shake well. Toss warm artichokes, beans and olives with dressing in large bowl. Cover; refrigerate 3 hours or overnight.

Serves 4 to 6.

■ Best made a day ahead.
■ Storage: Covered, in refrigerator.
■ Freeze: Not suitable.

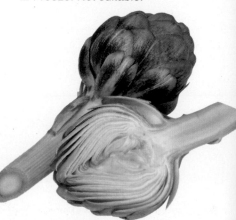

Globe Artichokes

Plate from Grace Bros; jug from Wednesdays Value Homeware

ARTICHOKES ALLA ROMANA WITH BASIL MAYONNAISE

4 medium artichokes
2 teaspoons olive oil
1 medium leek, sliced
1 small fresh red chili,
  finely chopped
6 slices mortadella, chopped
1/4 cup chopped fresh basil
3 tablespoons chopped fresh parsley
3 cups fresh breadcrumbs
1/2 cup grated parmesan cheese

BASIL MAYONNAISE
3 egg yolks
1 teaspoon stone ground mustard
10 fresh basil leaves
1 clove garlic, crushed
1 1/2 tablespoons lemon juice
1/2 cup olive oil

Boil, steam or microwave artichokes until just tender; drain. Remove and discard inner leaves and hairy choke.

Heat oil in large pan; cook leek, chili and mortadella, stirring, until leek is soft and mortadella almost crisp. Remove from heat; stir in herbs, breadcrumbs and cheese. Press breadcrumb stuffing between leaves and in center of each artichoke. Wrap bottom half of each artichoke in foil, leaving stuffing uncovered; place artichokes in single layer in baking dish. Bake, uncovered, in a 350ºF oven about 30 minutes or until tender and just browned. Just before serving, drizzle with Basil Mayonnaise.

Basil Mayonnaise: Blend or process egg yolks, mustard, basil, garlic and juice until smooth. With motor operating, gradually pour in oil; process until thick.

Serves 4.

■ Artichokes can be stuffed 3 hours ahead. Mayonnaise can be made a day ahead.
■ Storage: Covered, separately, in refrigerator.
■ Freeze: Not suitable.

LEFT: Artichokes alla Romana with Basil Mayonnaise.
OPPOSITE FROM TOP: Spanish-Style Jerusalem Artichoke Salad; Roasted Jerusalem Artichokes with Garlic; Char-Grilled Jerusalem Artichoke Salad.

Jerusalem artichokes

Plates, bowl and trivet from Wednesdays Value Homeware; tiles from Dorrus Ceramics

COOKING METHOD *Steaming works best for this root vegetable. Peel 2lb small Jerusalem artichokes; cook, covered, in a steamer basket over a pan of simmering water about 20 minutes or until just tender. Drain.*

ROASTED JERUSALEM ARTICHOKES WITH GARLIC

¼ cup olive oil
15 large Jerusalem artichokes
8 baby onions, quartered
1 medium bulb garlic, separated, unpeeled
2 sprigs fresh rosemary
¼ cup balsamic vinegar
3 tablespoons brown sugar

Heat oil in large flameproof baking dish; cook artichokes, onions and garlic, stirring, until onions are soft. Add remaining ingredients; cook, stirring, until sugar dissolves. Transfer dish to 375ºF oven; bake, uncovered, about 1 hour or until artichokes are tender, stirring occasionally.

Serves 4 to 6.

■ Best made just before serving.
■ Freeze: Not suitable.
■ Microwave: Not suitable.

CHAR-GRILLED JERUSALEM ARTICHOKE SALAD

12 medium Jerusalem artichokes, thinly sliced
3 tablespoons olive oil
2 medium sweet potatoes, thinly sliced
2 medium yellow bell peppers
2 medium red bell peppers

CHILI MINT DRESSING
1½ cups firmly packed fresh mint
½ cup cider vinegar
½ cup olive oil
¼ cup sweet chili sauce

Combine artichokes and oil in medium bowl; mix well.

Griddle-fry or barbecue artichoke and sweet potato slices, both sides, until just tender. Quarter bell peppers, discard seeds and membranes; grill or barbecue bell pepper pieces until skin blisters and blackens, peel away skin.

Gently toss vegetables with Chili Mint Dressing in large bowl.
Chili Mint Dressing: Blend or process all ingredients until smooth.

Serves 4 to 6.

■ Can be made 3 hours ahead.
■ Storage: Covered, in refrigerator.
■ Freeze: Not suitable.
■ Microwave: Not suitable.

SPANISH-STYLE JERUSALEM ARTICHOKE SALAD

12 medium Jerusalem artichokes
2 medium tomatoes
4oz arugula, trimmed
1 small red onion, sliced
1 cup black olives

SAFFRON PAPRIKA DRESSING
⅓ cup white vinegar
½ cup olive oil
1 clove garlic, crushed
¼ teaspoon saffron threads
¼ teaspoon sweet paprika
1 teaspoon sugar

Steam artichokes until just tender. Cut tomatoes into wedges. Gently toss artichokes, tomatoes and remaining ingredients with Saffron Paprika Dressing in large bowl.

Saffron Paprika Dressing: Combine all ingredients in jar; shake well.

Serves 4 to 6.

■ Salad best made just before serving. Saffron Paprika Dressing can be made a day ahead.
■ Storage: Covered, in refrigerator.
■ Freeze: Not suitable.
■ Microwave: Not suitable.

Jerusalem Artichokes

Arugula

Arugula, rocket, roquette, rucola, rugula – call it what you will, but this distinctive salad green will always answer back with spicy assertiveness. Arugula has launched onto today's table in a big way, and no wonder: whether used in cooking or served raw flaked with parmesan and drizzled with balsamic vinegar, it's a blast.

Arugula

ARUGULA SALAD WITH TOMATO VINAIGRETTE

3 tablespoons butter
2 cloves garlic, crushed
2oz pastrami, chopped
2 teaspoons brown sugar
2 cups fresh sourdough
    breadcrumbs
3 tablespoons chopped
    fresh cilantro
4oz arugula

TOMATO VINAIGRETTE
3 small tomatoes
1/4 cup white wine vinegar
2 teaspoons Worcestershire sauce
few drops Tabasco sauce
1 teaspoon sugar
1/3 cup olive oil

Heat butter in large pan; cook garlic and pastrami, stirring, until pastrami is crisp. Stir in sugar and breadcrumbs; cook, stirring, until breadcrumbs are browned. Remove from heat; stir in cilantro.

Just before serving, toss arugula in Tomato Vinaigrette in large bowl; sprinkle with breadcrumb mixture.

Tomato Vinaigrette: Blend or process tomatoes, vinegar, sauces and sugar until pureed. With motor operating, gradually pour in oil; process until smooth. Strain into jar.

Serves 6.

■ Salad must be made just before serving. Breadcrumbs and Tomato Vinaigrette can be made a day ahead.
■ Storage: Breadcrumbs in an airtight container. Vinaigrette, covered, in refrigerator.
■ Freeze: Not suitable.
■ Microwave: Not suitable.

ARUGULA CORNMEAL WEDGES

4 tablespoons butter
1 small leek, finely chopped
2 cloves garlic, crushed
1/3 cup all-purpose flour
3 tablespoons cornmeal
1 cup milk
4 eggs, separated
1/2 cup coarsely grated parmesan cheese
4oz arugula, chopped

Oil 9 x 12-inch baking pan; line with baking paper, extending paper 1-inch over edge of long sides of pan.

Heat butter in medium pan; cook leek and garlic, stirring, until leek is soft. Stir in flour and cornmeal gradually; cook, stirring, 1 minute. Remove from heat; gradually stir in milk. Return to heat; cook, stirring, until mixture boils and thickens. Remove from heat; stir in lightly beaten egg yolks, parmesan and arugula. Transfer mixture to large bowl.

Beat egg whites in small bowl with electric mixer until soft peaks form; fold into arugula cornmeal mixture in 2 batches. Spread mixture into prepared pan; bake, uncovered, in 400ºF oven about 12 minutes or until browned. Turn onto board; cut into wedges.

Serves 6.

■ Best made just before serving.
■ Freeze: Not suitable.
■ Microwave: Not suitable.

OPPOSITE: Arugula Salad with Tomato Vinaigrette.
ABOVE: Arugula Cornmeal Wedges.

Asian vegetables

Today's obsession with all manner of Asian cuisines naturally extends to a fascination with the beautifully unusual greens that so excited us in market places from Bombay to Beijing... so much so, in fact, that now we treat them with familiarity in our own kitchens.

Tat soi and Mustard greens

COOKING METHOD *Cooking times are based on 10 ounces tat soi or 1lb mustard greens, bases trimmed, leaves separated.*

• **BOIL** *Add tat soi or mustard greens to large pan of boiling water; boil, uncovered, about 3 minutes or until tender. Drain.*

• **STEAM** *Place tat soi or mustard greens in steamer basket; cook, covered, over pan of simmering water about 5 minutes or until tender. Drain.*

• **MICROWAVE** *Place tat soi or mustard greens and 1 tablespoon water in large microwave-safe dish. Cover, microwave on HIGH (100%) about 3 minutes or until tender, pausing halfway during cooking time to stir. Drain.*

Tested in an 830-watt oven

TAT SOI AND MUSTARD GREENS WITH PLUM SAUCE

1¹/₂ tablespoons peanut oil
4 cloves garlic, sliced
3 tablespoons finely sliced
   fresh ginger
1lb tat soi
1lb mustard greens
1¹/₂ tablespoons cornstarch
¹/₄ cup plum sauce
1¹/₂ tablespoons soy sauce
1¹/₂ tablespoons hoisin sauce

Heat oil in wok or large pan; stir-fry garlic and ginger until fragrant. Add tat soi and mustard greens then blended cornstarch and sauces; stir until sauce boils and thickens.

Serves 4 to 6.

■ Best made just before serving.
■ Freeze: Not suitable.
■ Microwave: Not suitable.

China from Waterford Wedgwood; tiles from Country Floors

Mustard Greens

Tat Soi

Choy sum

Choy Sum

Chinese Broccoli

COOKING METHODS *Cooking times are based on 2lb choy sum, ends trimmed, open flowers removed and discarded.*

• **BOIL** *Add choy sum to large pan of boiling water; boil, uncovered, about 4 minutes or until tender. Drain.*

• **STEAM** *Place choy sum in steamer basket; cook, covered, over pan of simmering water about 4 minutes or until tender. Drain.*

• **MICROWAVE** *Place choy sum and 1 tablespoon water in large microwave-safe dish. Cover, microwave on HIGH (100%) about 3 minutes or until tender, pausing halfway during cooking time to stir. Drain.*

Tested in an 830-watt oven

CHOY SUM IN LIME AND COCONUT

2 teaspoons cornstarch
1 teaspoon sugar
3 tablespoons lime juice
1 teaspoon fish sauce
2/3 cup coconut milk
2lb choy sum

Blend cornstarch and sugar with juice in wok or large pan; stir in sauce and milk. Stir until mixture boils and thickens. Add choy sum; stir until just wilted.

Serves 4.

■ Best made just before serving.
■ Freeze: Not suitable.
■ Microwave: Not suitable.

ABOVE FROM LEFT: Choy Sum in Lime and Coconut; Hunan Vegetable Stir-Fry.
OPPOSITE: Chinese Zucchini Omelette.

Chinese broccoli

COOKING METHODS *Cooking times are based on 2lb Chinese broccoli, trimmed, chopped.*

• **BOIL** *Add Chinese broccoli to large pan of boiling water; boil, uncovered, about 3 minutes or until tender. Drain.*

• **STEAM** *Place Chinese broccoli in steamer basket; cook, covered, over pan of simmering water about 4 minutes or until tender. Drain.*

• **MICROWAVE** *Place Chinese broccoli and 1 tablespoon water in large microwave-safe dish. Cover, microwave on HIGH (100%) about 3 minutes or until tender, pausing halfway during cooking time to stir. Drain.*

Tested in an 830-watt oven

HUNAN VEGETABLE STIR-FRY

2 teaspoons cornstarch
1/4 cup lime juice
3 tablespoons peanut oil
3 tablespoons sweet chili sauce
1 1/2 tablespoons fish sauce
2lb Chinese broccoli
**8oz can water chestnuts,
    drained, sliced**
8oz mung bean sprouts
**1/3 cup unsalted peanuts,
    toasted, chopped**

Blend cornstarch with juice in wok or large pan; stir in oil and sauces. Stir until mixture boils and thickens. Add remaining ingredients; stir-fry about 3 minutes or until broccoli is just tender.

Serves 4 to 6.

■ Best made just before serving.
■ Freeze: Not suitable.
■ Microwave: Not suitable.

Chinese zucchini

COOKING METHODS *Cooking times are based on 2lb Chinese zucchini, fuzz removed with a damp cloth, cut as required.*

• **BOIL** *Add Chinese zucchini to large pan of boiling water; boil, uncovered, about 6 minutes or until tender. Drain.*

• **STEAM** *Place Chinese zucchini in steamer basket; cook, covered, over pan of simmering water about 7 minutes or until just tender. Drain.*

• **MICROWAVE** *Place Chinese zucchini and 1 tablespoon water in large microwave-safe dish. Cover, microwave on HIGH (100%) about 5 minutes or until tender, pausing halfway during cooking time to stir. Drain.*

Tested in an 830-watt oven

CHINESE ZUCCHINI OMELETTE

1 medium Chinese zucchini
1 1/2 tablespoons peanut oil
1 small leek, finely chopped
2 cloves garlic, crushed
**1 medium red bell pepper, seeded,
    finely chopped**
2 slices bacon, finely chopped
8 eggs, lightly beaten
1/2 cup grated cheddar cheese

Slice zucchini in half lengthwise, remove and discard seeds; grate zucchini coarsely.

Heat oil in deep 12-inch pan; cook leek, garlic, bell pepper and bacon, stirring, until bell pepper is tender. Add eggs and half the cheese; cook over low heat until omelette has nearly set. Sprinkle top with remaining cheese; place omelette under heated broiler about 2 minutes or until top is browned.

Serves 6.

■ Best made just before serving.
■ Freeze: Not suitable.
■ Microwave: Not suitable.

Plate from Accoutrement

Chinese
Zucchini

Asian vegetables

Bok Choy

Wing Beans

Jug from Home & Garden on the Mall

Wing beans

COOKING METHODS *Cooking times are based on 1lb wing beans, trimmed.*

• **BOIL** *Add beans to large pan of boiling water; boil, uncovered, about 2 minutes or until tender. Drain.*

• **STEAM** *Place beans in steamer basket; cook, covered, over pan of simmering water about 2 minutes or until tender. Drain.*

• **MICROWAVE** *Place beans and 1 tablespoon water in large microwave-safe dish. Cover, microwave on HIGH (100%) about 4 minutes or until tender, pausing halfway during cooking time to stir. Drain.*

Tested in an 830-watt oven

WING BEANS IN PEANUT SAUCE

1lb wing beans
1/3 cup crunchy peanut butter
3 tablespoons sweet chili sauce
1 1/2 tablespoons lemon juice
2/3 cup chicken stock
2 teaspoons brown sugar
3 tablespoons coconut milk

Boil, steam or microwave beans until just tender; drain.

Combine remaining ingredients in wok or large pan; simmer about 5 minutes or until mixture thickens slightly. Add beans; stir-fry until hot.

Serves 4 to 6.

■ Best made just before serving.
■ Freeze: Suitable.

Bok choy

COOKING METHODS *Cooking times are based on 13/4lb baby bok choy, bases trimmed, leaves separated.*

• **BOIL** *Add bok choy to large pan of boiling water; boil, uncovered, about 2 minutes or until tender. Drain.*

• **STEAM** *Place bok choy in steamer basket; cook, covered, over pan of simmering water, about 3 minutes or until tender. Drain.*

• **MICROWAVE** *Place bok choy and 1 tablespoon water in large microwave-safe dish. Cover, microwave on HIGH (100%) about 3 minutes or until tender, pausing halfway during cooking time to stir. Drain.*

Tested in an 830-watt oven

SESAME BOK CHOY

2 teaspoons cornstarch
3 tablespoons water
3 tablespoons hoisin sauce
1 1/2 tablespoons oyster sauce
2 teaspoons soy sauce
2 teaspoons sesame oil
13/4lb baby bok choy
1 1/2 tablespoons sesame seeds, toasted

Blend cornstarch with water in small bowl; stir in sauces.

Heat oil in wok or large pan; stir-fry bok choy and seeds until bok choy is just tender. Stir in sauce mixture; stir until mixture boils and thickens.

Serves 4.

■ Best made just before serving.
■ Freeze: Not suitable.
■ Microwave: Suitable.

Chinese water spinach

COOKING METHODS *Cooking times are based on 6 ounces Chinese water spinach, bases trimmed, leaves separated.*

• **BOIL** *Add Chinese water spinach to large pan of boiling water; boil, uncovered, about 2 minutes or until tender. Drain.*

• **STEAM** *Place Chinese water spinach in steamer basket; cook, covered, over pan of simmering water, about 3 minutes or until tender. Drain.*

• **MICROWAVE** *Place Chinese water spinach and 1 tablespoon water in large microwave-safe dish. Cover, microwave on HIGH (100%) about 3 minutes or until tender, pausing halfway during cooking time to stir. Drain.*

Tested in an 830-watt oven

CHINESE WATER SPINACH WITH CRISPY NOODLES

12oz Chinese water spinach
2 stalks celery, finely sliced
8oz cherry tomatoes, halved
6 green onions, finely sliced
3oz can chow mein noodles
1/3 cup pecans, toasted, chopped

SOY AND CHILI DRESSING
1/4 cup peanut oil
3 tablespoons white vinegar
3 tablespoons sweet chili sauce
1 1/2 tablespoons soy sauce
1/2 teaspoon sesame oil

Combine all ingredients in large bowl with Soy and Chili Dressing; toss gently.
Soy and Chili Dressing: Combine all ingredients in jar; shake well.

Serves 6.

■ Soy and Chili Dressing can be made 3 days ahead. Recipe must be made just before serving.
■ Storage: Dressing, covered, in refrigerator.
■ Freeze: Not suitable.

Chinese Water Spinach

OPPOSITE: Sesame Bok Choy.
ABOVE LEFT: Chinese Water Spinach with Crispy Noodles.
LEFT: Wing Beans in Peanut Sauce.

Asparagus

Since there are few vegetables better than elegant fresh asparagus, it's one of life's great mysteries why so many people either overcook or ignore this tender young shoot belonging to the lily family. Whether you choose to cook the green or white variety, a handy rule of thumb to remember when judging readiness is that the tip droops slightly and the stem offers just the slightest resistance.

COOKING METHODS *Cooking times are based on 1lb asparagus, woody ends snapped off, lower part of stem peeled (from spear downward) with vegetable peeler if stems are thick.*

- **BOIL** *Add asparagus to large pan of boiling water; boil, uncovered, about 3 minutes or until tender. Drain.*

- **STEAM** *Place asparagus in steamer basket; cook, covered, over pan of simmering water about 4 minutes or until just tender. Drain.*

- **MICROWAVE** *Place asparagus and 2 tablespoons water in large microwave-safe dish. Cover, microwave on HIGH (100%) about 3 minutes or until tender. Drain.*

Tested in an 830-watt oven

ASPARAGUS SALAD WITH LEMON HERB VINAIGRETTE

2 teaspoons olive oil
3¹/₂ oz shaved smoked ham, chopped
2lb asparagus
2oz firm brie cheese, chopped
1 medium tomato seeded, chopped

LEMON HERB VINAIGRETTE
1¹/₂ tablespoons red wine vinegar
3 tablespoons lemon juice
¹/₃ cup light olive oil
1¹/₂ tablespoons chopped fresh chives
1¹/₂ tablespoons chopped fresh parsley

Heat oil in small pan; cook ham, stirring, until browned and crisp. Cool.

Boil, steam or microwave asparagus until just tender. Drain, then transfer to large bowl. Pour about three-quarters of Lemon Herb Vinaigrette over asparagus; gently toss to combine. Place asparagus on serving plate; scatter with ham, brie and tomato. Drizzle with remaining Lemon Herb Vinaigrette and serve immediately.

Lemon Herb Vinaigrette: Combine all ingredients in jar; shake well.

Serves 6 to 8.

■ Best made just before serving. Lemon Herb Vinaigrette can be made 3 days ahead.
■ Storage: Covered, in refrigerator.
■ Freeze: Not suitable.

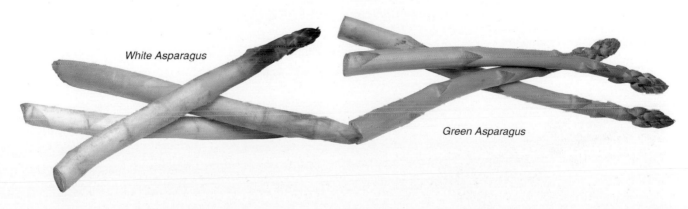

White Asparagus

Green Asparagus

Asparagus

China from Accoutrement; napkin and spoon from Home & Garden on the Mall

ASPARAGUS WITH THREE SAVORY BUTTERS

Asparagus is best cooked just before serving. Each of the butter recipes makes enough for 1¹/2lb asparagus, which serves 6. Savory butters can be made 3 days ahead and stored covered, separately, in refrigerator or frozen for up to 2 months.

1¹/2lb asparagus

Boil, steam or microwave asparagus until just tender; drain then transfer asparagus to large bowl. Add desired flavored butter; gently toss asparagus to coat in butter as it melts.

LEMON MUSTARD BUTTER

**6 tablespoons butter, softened
1¹/2 tablespoons stone ground
    mustard
1¹/2 tablespoons lemon juice
¹/4 teaspoon freshly cracked
    black pepper**

Combine all ingredients in small bowl; mix well.

SUN-DRIED TOMATO BUTTER

**2 teaspoons olive oil
¹/2 small red onion, finely chopped
2 teaspoons lemon juice
6 tablespoons butter, softened
3 tablespoons chopped drained
    sun-dried tomatoes in oil
1¹/2 tablespoons chopped
    fresh parsley**

Heat oil in small pan; cook onion, stirring, until soft and fragrant. Cool. Combine onion with remaining ingredients in small bowl; mix well.

HONEY NUT BUTTER

**6 tablespoons butter, softened
1¹/2 tablespoons chopped
    fresh cilantro
1¹/2 tablespoons honey
3 tablespoons chopped macadamia
    nuts, toasted
1 teaspoon mild curry powder
¹/2 teaspoon ground cumin**

Combine all ingredients in small bowl; mix well.

ASPARAGUS AND ARUGULA STIR-FRY

**1¹/2lb asparagus
3 tablespoons olive oil
2 cloves garlic, crushed
1 medium red bell pepper,
    seeded, sliced
3 tablespoons balsamic vinegar
3 tablespoons tomato paste
1¹/2 tablespoons water
4oz arugula**

Cut each asparagus spear into 3 pieces. Heat oil in wok or large pan; stir-fry asparagus, garlic and bell pepper until almost tender. Add combined vinegar, paste and water; stir-fry until asparagus is just tender. Add rocket; stir until just wilted.

Serves 4 to 6.

■ Best made just before serving.
■ Freeze: Not suitable.
■ Microwave: Not suitable.

*CLOCKWISE FROM TOP RIGHT:
Sun-Dried Tomato Butter; Lemon Mustard
Butter; Honey Nut Butter.
OPPOSITE: Asparagus and Arugula
Stir-Fry.*

Wurtz: A rather uncommon variety similar to the Fuerte but larger and more lemony with a freckled, lighter-green, smooth skin.

Hass: A definite pear-shape but an extremely thick neck. Deep purple to black bumpy skin; coarse yellow flesh and small seed. Slightly nutty, almost sweet flavor.

Sharwill: Ovoid in shape with a puckered, true-avocado colored skin and citrus-yellow flesh. Smoky, full flavor; luscious spreadable texture.

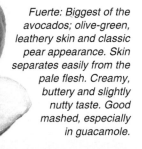

Fuerte: Biggest of the avocados; olive-green, leathery skin and classic pear appearance. Skin separates easily from the pale flesh. Creamy, buttery and slightly nutty taste. Good mashed, especially in guacamole.

Avocados

Vitamin-rich and cholesterol-free, the avocado is a nearly perfect food – how can it also taste as delicious as it does? One or more of the myriad varieties grown locally can be found year round, so the only limits to its use are those imposed by your imagination.

MEXICAN-STYLE BREAD SALAD

2 large pieces pita bread
1½ tablespoons olive oil
2 medium plum tomatoes
2 large avocados, sliced
11oz can corn kernels, rinsed, drained
11oz can kidney beans, rinsed, drained
½ small romaine lettuce

GARLIC AND CHILI DRESSING
¼ cup lemon juice
⅓ cup olive oil
2 cloves garlic, crushed
1 teaspoon sambal oelek
3 tablespoons sweet chili sauce

Brush pita both sides with oil, place on baking sheets; bake in a 375ºF oven about 15 minutes or until crisp. Cool; break into pieces.

Cut tomatoes in wedges; combine with avocados, corn and beans in large bowl. Just before serving, toss vegetable mixture with pita pieces and Garlic and Chili Dressing; place in lettuce-lined serving bowl.

Garlic and Chili Dressing: Combine all ingredients in jar; shake well.

Serves 6.

■ Pita and Garlic and Chili Dressing can be made a day ahead.
■ Storage: Pita, in airtight container. Dressing, covered, in refrigerator.
■ Freeze: Not suitable.
■ Microwave: Not suitable.

SPINACH, PAPAYA AND AVOCADO SALAD

1 bunch spinach
¼ cup pine nuts, toasted
1lb papaya, sliced
2 large avocados, sliced

TANGY ORANGE DRESSING
¼ cup light olive oil
¼ cup orange juice
1 teaspoon stone ground mustard
2 teaspoons balsamic vinegar

Combine all ingredients in large bowl; add Tangy Orange Dressing, mix gently.
Tangy Orange Dressing: Combine all ingredients in jar; shake well.

Serves 4.

■ Must be made just before serving.
■ Freeze: Not suitable.

CREAMY AVOCADO AND MANGO SALAD

1 cup mung bean sprouts
1/2 bunch watercress
1 medium avocado, sliced
2 stalks celery, sliced
1 medium mango, sliced

CREAMY AVOCADO DRESSING
1/2 small avocado
1/2 cup buttermilk
1 teaspoon stone ground mustard
1 1/2 tablespoons olive oil
1 1/2 tablespoons lemon juice
1 teaspoon wasabi paste

Combine all ingredients in large bowl; drizzle with Creamy Avocado Dressing.
Creamy Avocado Dressing: Blend or process all ingredients until smooth.
Serves 4.
■ Must be made just before serving.
■ Freeze: Not suitable.

OPPOSITE: Mexican-Style Bread Salad.
ABOVE FROM TOP: Creamy Avocado and Mango Salad; Spinach, Papaya and Avocado Salad.

Avocado Tips

■ Avocados are ripe if, when cradled in the palm of your hand, they yield to slight pressure. Don't prod an avocado with a finger unless you want to pierce the skin!

■ Black spots that appear in the flesh are caused by storage at cold temperatures: ripen avocados at room temperature if possible. They can be refrigerated for a maximum of 2 days in the least cold part of your refrigerator to slow the ripening process but any longer could cause them damage.

■ To hasten the ripening of avocados, seal them, along with a piece of apple, in a brown paper bag and leave in a warm corner of your kitchen.

■ When storing half a ripe avocado, leave the seed in and sprinkle with fresh lemon juice before covering.

Beans

Broad, round or flat; shelled or left podded; green, yellow or spotted – fresh beans of all descriptions are members of the same family, the legumes; dried, they are called pulses. Both ways, they constitute an internationally delicious force in both simple and more elegant cuisines.

Fava beans

COOKING METHODS *Cooking times are based on 2lb fava beans, removed from outer pods.*

- **BOIL** *Add fava beans to large pan of boiling water; boil, uncovered, 2 minutes. Drain then refresh under cold water; drain again.*

- **STEAM** *Place fava beans in steamer basket; cook, covered, over pan of simmering water, 5 minutes. Drain then refresh under cold water; drain again.*

- **MICROWAVE** *Place fava beans and 1/4 cup water in large microwave-safe bowl. Cover, microwave on HIGH (100%) about 6 minutes or until tender, pausing halfway during cooking time to stir. Drain then refresh under cold water; drain again.*
Tested in an 830-watt oven

CHILI BEANS WITH TOMATOES, OLIVES AND FETA

3lb fava beans, shelled
1 1/2 tablespoons olive oil
1 small red onion, thinly sliced
1 clove garlic, crushed
1 small fresh red chili, chopped
3 medium tomatoes, peeled, seeded, chopped
1/2 cup dry white wine
3 tablespoons tomato paste
1/3 cup kalamata olives
2 teaspoons balsamic vinegar
2 teaspoons lemon juice
2 teaspoons sugar
8oz feta cheese, chopped
3 tablespoons chopped fresh Italian parsley

Boil, steam or microwave beans until tender. Drain; refresh under cold water, then remove and discard outer skins.

Heat oil in medium pan; cook onion, garlic and chili, stirring, until onion is soft. Add tomatoes, wine, paste, olives, vinegar, juice and sugar; simmer, uncovered, about 8 minutes or until thickened. Gently stir in beans, feta and half the parsley. Just before serving, sprinkle with remaining parsley.

Serves 4 to 6.

■ Best made on day of serving.
■ Freeze: Not suitable.

FAVA BEAN AND POTATO GRATIN

2lb fava beans, shelled
5 medium potatoes
2 tablespoons butter
3 tablespoons all-purpose flour
2 cups milk
2 teaspoons chicken stock base or 2 chicken bouillon cubes
1 clove garlic, crushed
1/3 cup grated cheddar cheese
2 teaspoons chopped fresh thyme
1 1/2 tablespoons grated parmesan cheese

Boil, steam or microwave beans until tender. Drain; refresh under cold water, then remove and discard outer skins. Cut potatoes into 1-inch pieces; cook in large pan of boiling water, uncovered, until just tender. Drain.

Melt butter in small pan; add flour, stir over heat until bubbling. Remove from heat; gradually stir in milk until mixture boils and thickens. Stir in stock paste, garlic, cheddar and half the thyme; cook 1 minute.

Combine beans and potatoes in a shallow 6-cup ovenproof dish; pour sauce over the vegetables. Scatter combined parmesan and remaining thyme over top; bake, uncovered, in 350ºF oven about 35 minutes or until browned lightly.

Serves 6.

■ Best made on day of serving.
■ Freeze: Not suitable.

OPPOSITE FROM TOP:
Fava Bean and Potato Gratin;
Chili Beans with Tomatoes, Olives and Feta.

Fava Beans

Long beans

COOKING METHODS
Cooking times are based on 1lb long beans, cut into 4-inch lengths.

• **BOIL** *Add long beans to large pan of boiling water; boil, uncovered, about 5 minutes or until tender. Drain.*

• **STEAM** *Place long beans in steamer basket; cook, covered, over pan of simmering water about 5 minutes or until tender. Drain.*

• **MICROWAVE** *Place long beans and 1 tablespoon water in large microwave-safe dish. Cover, microwave on HIGH (100%) about 5 minutes or until tender, pausing halfway during cooking time to stir. Stand 1 minute before serving. Drain.*

Tested in an 850-watt oven

LONG BEAN, HAZELNUT AND ROASTED PEPPER SALAD

1lb long beans or green beans
2 large red bell peppers, quartered, roasted
1/2 cup hazelnuts, toasted, chopped roughly
1/4 cup orange juice
1/4 cup olive oil
1 1/2 tablespoons white wine vinegar
1 teaspoon grated orange rind
1 teaspoon sugar
1/4 teaspoon cracked black pepper
1/4 teaspoon salt

Cut beans into 3-inch lengths. Boil, steam or microwave until just tender; drain. Slice the pepper pieces thinly. Gently toss beans, peppers and nuts with combined remaining ingredients in medium bowl.

Serves 6.

■ Best made just before serving.
■ Freeze: Not suitable.

Snake Beans

CILANTRO PESTO LONG BEANS

1lb long beans
3 medium plum tomatoes, seeded, finely chopped
1 1/2 tablespoons pine nuts, toasted
1/4 cup parmesan cheese, shaved

CILANTRO PESTO
4oz fresh cilantro
3 tablespoons pine nuts, toasted
1 clove garlic, chopped
1/4 cup grated parmesan cheese
1/4 cup olive oil

Cut beans into 2-inch lengths. Boil, steam or microwave beans until just tender; drain.

Gently toss beans, tomatoes, nuts and half the parmesan with Cilantro Pesto in medium bowl. Just before serving, sprinkle with the remaining parmesan.

Cilantro Pesto: Remove and discard roots from cilantro. Blend or process cilantro, nuts, garlic and parmesan until almost smooth. With motor operating, gradually pour in oil; process until smooth.

Serves 6.

■ Best made just before serving. Cilantro Pesto can be made a day ahead.
■ Storage: Covered, in refrigerator.
■ Freeze: Not suitable.

Green beans

COOKING METHODS *Cooking times are based on 1lb green beans, trimmed as desired.*

- **BOIL** *Add green beans to large pan of boiling water; boil, uncovered, about 5 minutes or until tender. Drain.*

- **STEAM** *Place green beans in steamer basket; cook, covered, over pan of simmering water about 6 minutes or until tender. Drain.*

- **MICROWAVE** *Place green beans and 2 tablespoons water in microwave-safe dish. Cover, microwave on HIGH (100%) about 4 minutes or until tender, pausing halfway during cooking time to stir. Stand 1 minute before serving. Drain.*

Tested in an 850-watt oven

ROMAN-STYLE GREEN BEANS

3 slices prosciutto
1lb green beans
3 tablespoons olive oil
8oz button mushrooms
3 tablespoons pine nuts, toasted
1½ tablespoons lemon juice
6 sprigs fresh lemon thyme

Place prosciutto under broiler until crisp; drain on paper towels. Snap prosciutto into small pieces; reserve. Trim stem ends of beans only.

Heat oil in wok or large pan; stir-fry mushrooms 1 minute. Add beans; stir-fry about 3 minutes or until just tender. Add prosciutto, nuts, juice and thyme; toss mixture gently until heated through.

Serves 4 to 6.

■ Best made just before serving.
■ Freeze: Not suitable.
■ Microwave: Not suitable.

Bowls and platter from Home & Garden on the Mall; napkins and salad servers from The Bay Tree Kitchen Shop

Green (French) Beans

ABOVE
FROM TOP:
Cilantro Pesto
Long Beans;
Long Bean,
Hazelnut and Roasted
Pepper Salad.
RIGHT: Roman-Style Green Beans.

Beans

CHAR-GRILLED POTATO, BEAN AND OLIVE SALAD

1lb butter beans, trimmed
1lb tiny new potatoes, halved
2 tablespoons olive oil
1/2 cup black olives
**1/3 cup roughly chopped
   fresh mint**

SWEET CHILI DRESSING
3 tablespoons lemon juice
3 tablespoons olive oil
3 tablespoons sweet chili sauce

Boil, steam or microwave beans and potatoes, separately, until just tender; drain. Rinse beans under cold water; drain. Brush potatoes with oil; cook on heated oiled griddle pan or barbecue, cut-side down, until browned lightly and just tender. Gently mix beans, potatoes, olives and mint with Sweet Chili Dressing in large bowl.
Sweet Chili Dressing: Combine all ingredients in jar; shake well.

Serves 6.

■ Best made just before serving. Sweet Chili Dressing can be made a day ahead.
■ Storage: Covered, in refrigerator.
■ Freeze: Not suitable.

MIDDLE-EASTERN BEAN SALAD

8oz butter beans
8oz green beans
**1 tablespoon sumac [see Glossary]
   or tamarind concentrate**
1 small red onion, finely chopped
**1/3 cup roughly chopped fresh
   Italian parsley**
1/4 cup lemon juice
3 tablespoons olive oil
1 1/2 tablespoons honey
1 clove garlic, crushed

Boil, steam or microwave beans until almost tender. Rinse under cold water; drain. Gently mix beans with sumac or tamarind, onion, parsley and combined remaining ingredients in large bowl.

Serves 6.

■ Best made just before serving.
■ Freeze: Not suitable.

Salad bowl and plates from The Bay Tree Kitchen Shop

Butter beans

COOKING METHODS *Cooking times are based on 1lb butter beans, trimmed.*

• **BOIL** *Add beans to large pan of boiling water; boil, uncovered, about 5 minutes or until tender. Drain.*

• **STEAM** *Place beans in steamer basket; cook, covered, over pan of simmering water about 6 minutes or until tender. Drain.*

• **MICROWAVE** *Place beans and 2 tablespoons water in large microwave-safe dish. Cover, microwave on HIGH (100%) about 4 minutes or until tender, pausing halfway during cooking time to stir. Stand 1 minute before serving. Drain.*

Tested in an 850-watt oven

PAPRIKA TOMATO BEANS

1lb butter beans, trimmed
1 1/2 tablespoons olive oil
3 green onions, chopped
2 cloves garlic, crushed
1 1/2 teaspoons sweet paprika
1/4 cup tomato puree

Boil, steam or microwave beans until just tender; drain. Heat oil in large pan; cook onions and garlic 1 minute. Add paprika; cook 30 seconds. Stir in beans and puree until just heated through.

Serves 4 to 6.

■ Best made just before serving.
■ Freeze: Not suitable.

Butter Beans

*ABOVE LEFT: Paprika Tomato Beans.
OPPOSITE FROM TOP: Char-Grilled Potato, Bean and Olive Salad; Middle-Eastern Bean Salad.*

Cranberry beans

COOKING METHODS *Cooking times are based on 2lb cranberry beans, shelled.*

• **BOIL** *Add cranberry beans to large pan of boiling water; boil, uncovered, about 20 minutes or until tender. Drain.*

• **STEAM** *Place cranberry beans in steamer basket; cook, covered, over pan of simmering water about 30 minutes or until tender. Drain.*

• **MICROWAVE** *Place cranberry beans and 2 tablespoons water in large microwave safe dish. Cover, microwave on HIGH (100%) about 15 minutes or until tender, pausing halfway during cooking time to stir. Stand 1 minute before serving. Drain.*

Tested in an 850-watt oven

Cranberry Beans

BACON AND BEAN CASSEROLE

1 1/2 tablespoons vegetable oil
2 large onions, chopped
4 slices bacon, chopped
2 14oz cans tomatoes, undrained, crushed
1 cup water
1 teaspoon chicken stock base or chicken bouillon cube
1/4 cup Worcestershire sauce
2 teaspoons Dijon mustard
2lb cranberry beans, shelled

Heat oil in large heavy-based pan; cook onions and bacon, stirring, until both are browned lightly. Add remaining ingredients; bring to boil, simmer, covered, about 1 hour or until beans are tender, stirring occasionally.

Serves 6 to 8.

■ Can be made a day ahead.
■ Storage: Covered, in refrigerator.
■ Freeze: Suitable.
■ Microwave: Suitable.

CRANBERRY AND RED LENTIL DAL

3 tablespoons ghee or clarified butter
1 1/2 tablespoons black mustard seeds
1/2 teaspoon black onion seeds (kalonji)
1 tablespoon cumin seeds
10 curry leaves, torn
2 medium onions, chopped
3 cloves garlic, crushed
1 1/2 tablespoons grated fresh ginger
1 small fresh red chili, seeded, chopped
1 1/2 tablespoons ground coriander
1 teaspoon ground turmeric
2 14oz cans tomatoes, undrained, crushed
2 1/2 cups vegetable stock
1 cup red lentils, rinsed
2lb cranberry beans, shelled
1/3 cup cream
1/4 cup chopped fresh cilantro

Heat ghee in large heavy-based pan; cook seeds and curry leaves, stirring, until fragrant. Add onions, garlic, ginger and chili; cook, stirring, until onions are soft. Stir in ground spices; cook, stirring, 1 minute. Add tomatoes, stock, lentils and beans; cook, covered, over low heat, about 1 hour or until beans are tender. Just before serving, stir in cream and half the cilantro; when heated through, sprinkle with the remaining cilantro.

Serves 6 to 8.

■ Can be prepared a day ahead.
■ Storage: Covered, in refrigerator.
■ Freeze: Suitable.
■ Microwave: Suitable.

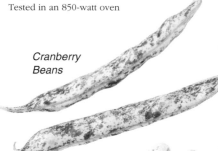

1 hour or until tomatoes are soft. Cover with foil if over browning.

Blend or process cooked vegetables with tomato paste and enough stock to make a smooth sauce.

Boil, steam or microwave beans until tender; drain. Place beans in serving bowl; spoon sauce over beans, sprinkle with parmesan and basil.

Serves 6 to 8.

■ Best made just before serving. Sauce can be made a day ahead; reheat before using.
■ Storage: Covered, in refrigerator.
■ Freeze: Not suitable.

ITALIAN BEANS WITH RED PEPPER PESTO

2lb Italian beans

PEPPER PESTO
**2 large red bell peppers,
  quartered, roasted
3/4 cup grated parmesan cheese
1 clove garlic, chopped
2/3 cup roughly chopped
    fresh basil
1/4 cup olive oil**

Boil, steam or microwave beans until tender; drain. Combine beans with pepper pesto in large bowl; mix well.
Pepper Pesto: Blend or process peppers, cheese, garlic and basil until finely chopped. With motor operating, gradually pour in oil; process until combined.

Serves 6 to 8.

■ Best made just before serving. Pepper Pesto can be made a day ahead.
■ Storage: Covered, in refrigerator.
■ Freeze: Not suitable.

Italian beans

COOKING METHODS *Cooking times are based on 2lb Italian beans, halved.*

• **BOIL** *Add Italian beans to large pan of boiling water; boil, uncovered, about 5 minutes or until tender. Drain.*

• **STEAM** *Place Italian beans in steamer basket; cook, covered, over pan of simmering water about 5 minutes or until tender. Drain.*

• **MICROWAVE** *Place Italian beans and 2 tablespoons water in large microwave-safe dish. Cover, microwave on HIGH (100%) about 5 minutes or until tender, pausing halfway through cooking time to stir. Stand 1 minute before serving. Drain.*

Tested in an 850-watt oven

ITALIAN BEANS WITH TOMATO AND GARLIC SAUCE

**12 large plum tomatoes
2 medium onions, quartered
8 cloves garlic, peeled
1/2 teaspoon sea salt
1/2 teaspoon cracked black pepper
3 tablespoons olive oil
2 tablespoons tomato paste
1/4 cup vegetable stock,
    approximately
1 1/2lb Italian beans, halved
1/4 cup parmesan cheese, shaved
1/4 cup loosely packed fresh
    basil, shredded**

Quarter tomatoes lengthwise; place tomatoes, cut-side up, in large baking dish, with onions and garlic. Sprinkle with salt and pepper, drizzle with oil; bake, uncovered, in 350ºF oven, about

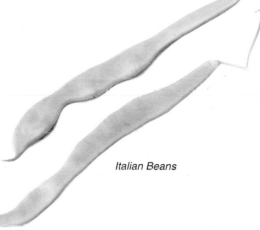

Italian Beans

*OPPOSITE TOP: Bacon and Bean Casserole.
OPPOSITE: Cranberry and Red Lentil Dal.
ABOVE FROM TOP: Italian Beans with Red Pepper Pesto; Italian Beans with Tomato and Garlic Sauce.*

29

Beets

Proof that opposites attract: the combination of a beet's outrageous color and subtle sweet taste has resulted in the vegetable's astonishing popularity today, both in home and restaurant kitchens.

COOKING METHODS
Cooking times are based on 3 medium beets, unpeeled, with 1 inch of stem remaining.

- **BOIL** *Add beets to medium pan of boiling water; boil, uncovered, about 45 minutes or until tender. Drain; peel while still warm.*

- **STEAM** *Place beets in steamer basket; cook, covered, over pan of simmering water about 55 minutes or until tender. Drain; peel beets while still warm.*

- **MICROWAVE** *Place beets and 2 tablespoons water in large microwave-safe dish. Cover, microwave on HIGH (100%) about 30 minutes or until tender, pausing halfway during cooking time to turn. Drain; peel while still warm.*

Tested in an 830-watt oven

BEET AND POTATO PUREE

4 medium beets
3 medium potatoes
3 tablespoons cream
1/2 teaspoon sugar
4 tablespoons butter

Boil, steam or microwave beets and potatoes, separately, until tender; drain, peel while warm. Coarsely chop beets and potatoes; blend or process with remaining ingredients until pureed.

Serves 4 to 6.

■ Best made just before serving.
■ Freeze: Not suitable.

BEET SKEWERS

You need 8 metal or sturdy bamboo skewers, each approximately 8-10 inches in length, for this recipe. Buy similar-sized potatoes to make the finished dish look more attractive.

3 medium beets, peeled
4 tiny new potatoes,
  unpeeled, halved
2 small onions, quartered
1 1/2 tablespoons olive oil
3 tablespoons maple syrup
1/4 cup cider vinegar
1 teaspoon grated orange rind
3 tablespoons orange juice
1 1/2 tablespoons chopped
  fresh mint

Quarter each beet; halve each quarter crosswise. Thread 3 pieces of beet onto 1 skewer, separating with 1 piece each of potato and onion; brush skewered vegetables with oil. Place skewers in single layer in large baking dish; bake, uncovered, in 350ºF oven about 35 minutes or until vegetables are tender, turning twice during cooking.

Combine syrup, vinegar, rind and juice in small pan. Bring to boil; simmer, uncovered, about 5 minutes or until thickened slightly. Pour syrup mixture over skewers; sprinkle with mint.

Serves 4.

■ Best made just before serving.
■ Freeze: Not suitable.
■ Microwave: Not suitable.

OPPOSITE FROM TOP: Beet and Potato Puree; Beet Skewers.

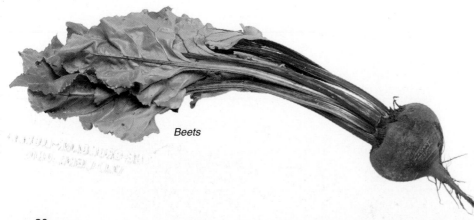

Beets

Belgian endive

Grown in the dark to retain its pale color and singular bittersweet taste, elegant Belgian endive – also known as witloo, witlof or even chicory – creates a frisson of flavor once exposed to the light of the myriad delicious ways it can be eaten, raw or cooked.

China from Villeroy & Boch

BELGIAN ENDIVE AU GRATIN

6 medium Belgian endives
4 tablespoons butter, chopped
1½ tablespoons brown sugar
½ teaspoon cracked black pepper
½ teaspoon sea salt
3 tablespoons all-purpose flour
1⅓ cups milk
⅓ cup cream
⅓ cup finely grated
   parmesan cheese
2 teaspoons packaged breadcrumbs

Belgian endive

Place endives in 6-cup shallow oven-proof dish; dot endives with half the butter, sprinkle with sugar, pepper and salt. Bake, covered, in 350ºF oven, 1½ hours. Uncover; bake 20 minutes or until endives are soft. Drain and discard juices from dish.

Meanwhile, heat remaining butter in small pan. Stir in flour; cook, stirring, until bubbling. Remove from heat, gradually stir in milk; stir over heat until mixture boils and thickens. Stir in cream and half the parmesan. Pour sauce over endives; sprinkle with combined remaining parmesan and breadcrumbs. Bake, uncovered, in 400ºF oven about 20 minutes or until browned lightly. Let rest 5 minutes before serving.

Serves 6.

■ Best made just before serving.
■ Freeze: Not suitable.
■ Microwave: Sauce suitable.

BELGIAN ENDIVE SALAD

4 medium Belgian endives
1½ tablespoons olive oil
3 bacon slices, finely chopped
2 small leeks, finely sliced
3 medium zucchini, finely sliced
**11oz can corn kernels,
    rinsed, drained**
4oz mesclun [see Lettuce]
¼ cup chopped fresh Italian parsley
3 hard-boiled eggs, quartered

DIJON DRESSING
¼ cup olive oil
3 tablespoons Dijon mustard
3 tablespoons lemon juice
1½ tablespoons mayonnaise
1½ teaspoons sugar
1 teaspoon balsamic vinegar

Trim and discard 1-inch off each endive base; separate leaves.

Heat oil in large pan, cook bacon, stirring, 1 minute. Add leeks and zucchini; cook, stirring, about 5 minutes, or until vegetables are tender. Cool.

Gently toss endive, vegetable mixture, corn, mesclun and parsley with half the dressing in large serving bowl. Place eggs on top of salad; drizzle with remaining dressing.

Dijon Dressing: Combine all ingredients in jar; shake well.

Serves 6.

■ Best made just before serving.
■ Freeze: Not suitable.

OPPOSITE: Belgian Endive Au Gratin.
ABOVE: Belgian Endive Salad.

35

Yellow
Bell Pepper

Green
Bell Pepper

Red Bell
Pepper

Purple Bell
Pepper

RIGHT FROM TOP: Bell Pepper, Garbanzo and Olive Salad; Roasted Bell Peppers with Port and Basil Dressing.
OPPOSITE: Grilled Bell Peppers with Arugula Pesto.

ROASTED BELL PEPPERS WITH PORT AND BASIL DRESSING

2 medium red bell peppers
2 medium green bell peppers
2 medium yellow bell peppers
10 green onions
8 cloves garlic
4 small onions, quartered
1¹/₂ tablespoons olive oil

PORT AND BASIL DRESSING
¹/₂ cup olive oil
¹/₄ cup balsamic vinegar
2 cloves garlic
¹/₃ cup firmly packed
   fresh basil
1¹/₂ tablespoons port
1¹/₂ tablespoons mild chili sauce

Quarter bell peppers; remove and discard seeds and membranes. Combine with remaining ingredients in large baking dish; bake, uncovered, in 350ºF oven 1 hour. Drizzle with Port and Basil Dressing while still warm.

Port and Basil Dressing: Blend or process all ingredients until pureed.

Serves 6 to 8.

■ Best made just before serving.
■ Freeze: Not suitable.
■ Microwave: Not suitable.

Bell peppers

Columbus is responsible for the confusion over this food's name, erroneously naming it a pepper when he took it from the New World to Europe. It's really a large, mild member of the chili family – but, by any other name, is just as delectably sweet.

BELL PEPPER, GARBANZO AND OLIVE SALAD

3/4 cup dried garbanzos
2 medium red bell peppers, seeded, chopped
2 medium green bell peppers, seeded, chopped
1 medium red onion, chopped
1/3 cup fresh Italian parsley
3/4 cup black olives

LEMON DRESSING
1/3 cup olive oil
1 medium onion, chopped
2 cloves garlic, crushed
2 teaspoons ground cumin
1 teaspoon hot paprika
1/4 cup lemon juice

Cover garbanzos with cold water in medium bowl; let stand overnight.

Drain garbanzos; rinse under cold water. Place garbanzos in large pan of boiling water; simmer, uncovered, about 45 minutes or until just tender. Drain; rinse under cold water until cool. Drain well then toss garbanzos with remaining ingredients and Lemon Dressing in large bowl.
Lemon Dressing: Heat 1 1/2 tablespoons of the oil in small pan; cook onion, garlic and spices, stirring, until onion is soft. Blend or process onion mixture with remaining oil and juice until smooth.

Serves 4 to 6.

■ Best made just before serving.
■ Freeze: Not suitable.
■ Microwave: Garbanzos suitable.

GRILLED BELL PEPPERS WITH ARUGULA PESTO

3 medium red bell peppers
3 medium yellow bell peppers
1/3 cup roasted macadamias, chopped

ARUGULA PESTO
2oz arugula, trimmed
1/4 cup grated parmesan cheese
1 clove garlic
1/4 cup macadamias, toasted, roughly chopped
1/2 cup olive oil

Quarter bell peppers; remove and discard seeds and membranes. Roast under broiler or in very hot oven, skin-side up, until skin blisters and blackens. Cover bell pepper pieces in plastic or paper for 5 minutes; peel away skin. Slice pieces in half lengthwise; gently toss with nuts and Arugula Pesto in serving bowl.
Arugula Pesto: Blend or process all ingredients until pureed.

Serves 4 to 6.

■ Best made just before serving.
■ Freeze: Not suitable.
■ Microwave: Not suitable.

Plate from Villeroy & Boch

Broccoli

One maligned, the other virtually unknown, broccoli and broccoflower deserve better reputations. Excellent sources of Vitamin C, available all year, and edible raw or cooked, their respective flavors are distinctively delicious.

Broccoli

COOKING METHODS *Cooking times are based on 1lb broccoli, cut into florets.*

• **BOIL** *Add broccoli to medium pan of boiling water; boil, uncovered, about 3 minutes or until tender. Drain.*

• **STEAM** *Place broccoli in single layer in steamer basket; cook, covered, over pan of simmering water about 7 minutes or until tender. Drain.*

• **MICROWAVE** *Place broccoli and ¼ cup water in medium microwave-safe dish. Cover, microwave on HIGH (100%) about 5 minutes or until tender, pausing halfway during cooking time to stir. Drain.*

Tested in an 850-watt oven

BROCCOLI WITH CHEESE AND BACON TOPPING

1½lb broccoli
3 slices bacon, chopped
3 tablespoons butter
¼ cup all-purpose flour
1 teaspoon stone ground mustard
⅓ cup dry white wine
1¼ cups milk
½ cup grated gruyere cheese
½ cup grated cheddar cheese
3 tablespoons grated
  parmesan cheese

Boil, steam or microwave broccoli until just tender; drain. Cook bacon, stirring, in small dry pan until browned; drain on paper towel.

Melt butter in medium pan; add flour, stir over heat until bubbling. Remove from heat; gradually stir in mustard, wine and milk. Stir over heat until sauce boils and thickens; remove from heat, stir in cheeses.

Stand broccoli upright in shallow oiled 6-cup ovenproof dish; pour over cheese mixture, scatter bacon over top. Cook under broiler about 5 minutes or until browned and heated through.

Serves 4 to 6.

■ Best made just before serving.
■ Freeze: Not suitable.
■ Microwave: Sauce suitable.

Broccoflower

Broccoli

Broccoflower

COOKING METHODS *Cooking times are based on 1lb broccoflower, cut into florets.*

• **BOIL** *Add broccoflower to medium pan of boiling water; boil, uncovered, about 3 minutes or until tender. Drain.*

• **STEAM** *Place broccoflower in single layer in steamer basket; cook, covered, over pan of simmering water about 4 minutes or until tender. Drain.*

• **MICROWAVE** *Place broccoflower and ¼ cup water in large microwave-safe dish. Cover, microwave on HIGH (100%) about 3 minutes or until tender, pausing halfway during cooking time to stir. Drain.*

Tested in an 850-watt oven

BROCCOLI, BROCCOFLOWER AND CAULIFLOWER STIR-FRY

4 tablespoons olive oil
1 medium red onion,
    cut into wedges
1lb broccoli florets, sliced
1lb broccoflower florets, sliced
1lb cauliflower florets, sliced
¼ cup cider vinegar
2 cloves garlic, crushed
1½ tablespoons brown sugar
¼ cup chopped fresh basil

Heat oil in wok or large pan; cook onion, stirring, until soft. Add florets; cook, stirring, 2 minutes. Add combined remaining ingredients; cook, stirring gently, about 2 minutes or until florets are just tender.

Serves 6.

■ Best made just before serving.
■ Freeze: Not suitable.
■ Microwave: Not suitable.

BROCCOFLOWER WITH BLUE CHEESE AND PECANS

1lb broccoflower florets
2 tablespoons butter
1 medium onion, finely chopped
½ cup dry white wine
½ cup cream
4oz creamy blue cheese, chopped
2 teaspoons cornstarch
1½ tablespoons water
3 tablespoons chopped pecans

Boil, steam or microwave broccoflower until just tender; drain.

Heat butter in medium pan; cook onion, stirring, until soft. Add wine; simmer, uncovered, about 2 minutes or until wine reduces slightly. Add cream and cheese; stir over low heat until

cheese melts. Add blended cornstarch and water; cook, stirring, until sauce boils and thickens.

Place broccoflower in 4-cup oven-proof dish. Pour the sauce over top, sprinkle with nuts. Bake, uncovered, in 375°F oven about 15 minutes or until browned.

Serves 4.

■ Best made just before serving.
■ Freeze: Not suitable.
■ Microwave: Sauce suitable.

OPPOSITE: Broccoli with Cheese and Bacon Topping.
ABOVE: Broccoli, Broccoflower and Cauliflower Stir-Fry.
BELOW: Broccoflower with Blue Cheese and Pecans.

Brussels sprouts

Members of the cabbage family, and resembling minuscule heads of cabbage too, Brussels sprouts were first cultivated in Belgium. Cultivate your taste for them by leaving in some of the crunch when cooking these nutty, sweet morsels.

COOKING METHODS *Cooking times are based on 2lb Brussels sprouts.*

- **BOIL** *Add Brussels sprouts to large pan of boiling water; boil, uncovered, about 8 minutes or until tender. Drain.*

- **STEAM** *Place Brussels sprouts in single layer in steamer basket; cook, covered, over pan of simmering water about 10 minutes or until tender. Drain.*

- **MICROWAVE** *Place Brussels sprouts and 1/4 cup water in large microwave-safe dish. Cover, microwave on HIGH (100%) about 8 minutes or until tender, pausing halfway during cooking time to stir. Drain.*
Tested in an 850-watt oven

HONEY ORANGE BRUSSELS SPROUTS

2lb Brussels sprouts
3 tablespoons orange juice
3 tablespoons stone ground mustard
1 1/2 tablespoons honey

Halve sprouts lengthwise. Boil, steam or microwave until just tender; drain. Gently toss sprouts with combined remaining ingredients in serving bowl.

Serves 4 to 6.

■ Best made just before serving.
■ Freeze: Not suitable.

BRUSSELS SPROUTS WITH BACON AND BREADCRUMBS

2lb Brussels sprouts
8 tablespoons butter
3 slices bacon, chopped
2 cups fresh breadcrumbs
4 green onions, chopped
1 1/2 tablespoons chopped fresh oregano
1 1/2 tablespoons chopped fresh basil
1 1/2 tablespoons chopped fresh thyme

Boil, steam or microwave sprouts until just tender; drain. Add about a third of the butter; mix well.

Heat remaining butter in large pan; cook bacon, stirring, until crisp. Add breadcrumbs; cook, stirring, until browned lightly. Add onions, herbs and sprouts; stir until heated through.

Serves 4 to 6.

■ Best made just before serving.
■ Freeze: Not suitable.

BRUSSELS SPROUT AND PEPPER MELANGE

2lb Brussels sprouts
3 tablespoons olive oil
2 medium onions, sliced
1 medium red bell pepper, seeded, chopped
1 medium yellow bell pepper, seeded, chopped
2 small fresh red chilies, chopped
4 tablespoons butter
3 tablespoons brown sugar
1/3 cup pine nuts, toasted

Boil, steam or microwave sprouts until just tender; drain.

Heat oil in large pan; cook onions, stirring, until soft. Add peppers and chilies; cook, stirring, until soft. Add butter and sugar; cook, stirring, until sugar has dissolved. Add pine nuts and sprouts; stir until heated through.

Serves 4 to 6.

■ Best made just before serving.
■ Freeze: Not suitable.

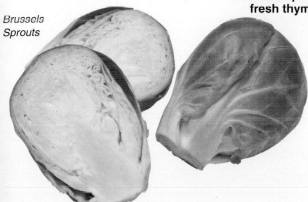

Brussels Sprouts

CLOCKWISE FROM TOP: Brussels Sprout and Pepper Melange; Brussels Sprouts with Bacon and Breadcrumbs; Honey Orange Brussels Sprouts.

Cabbages

Regardless of continent or culture, cabbage lifts its head in innumerable rustic soups, salads and casseroles. Traditionally a peasant food, grown in the harshest of climates and poorest of soils, it also has the capability of transforming itself, with the help of a keen cook, into many tasty dishes, good enough to set before a king.

SUMMERTIME CABBAGE SALAD

1lb red cabbage, shredded
12oz savoy cabbage, shredded
1 small red bell pepper,
  seeded, sliced
1 small yellow bell pepper,
  seeded, sliced
4 green onions, chopped
½ cup pine nuts, toasted

TANGY HERB DRESSING
1½ tablespoons tomato paste
1½ tablespoons lemon juice
3 tablespoons balsamic vinegar
3 tablespoons water
⅓ cup light olive oil
2 cloves garlic, crushed
3 tablespoons chopped
  fresh cilantro

Combine all ingredients in large bowl; toss gently with Tangy Herb Dressing.
Tangy Herb Dressing: Combine all ingredients in jar; shake well.

COOKING METHODS *Cooking times are based on 2lb cabbage, coarsely chopped.*

• **BOIL** *Add cabbage to large pan of boiling water; boil, uncovered, about 9 minutes or until tender. Drain.*

• **STEAM** *Place cabbage in steamer basket; cook, covered, over pan of simmering water about 12 minutes or until tender. Drain.*

• **MICROWAVE** *Place cabbage and 2 tablespoons water in large microwave-safe dish. Cover, microwave on HIGH (100%) about 9 minutes or until tender, pausing halfway during cooking time to stir. Drain.*

Tested in an 850-watt oven

Red Cabbage

42

Serves 6 to 8.

- Summertime Cabbage Salad best assembled just before serving. Tangy Herb Dressing can be made a day ahead.
- Storage: Covered, in refrigerator.
- Freeze: Not suitable.

BRAISED RED CABBAGE

4 tablespoons butter
2lb red cabbage, chopped
2 teaspoons red wine vinegar
1/4 cup redcurrant jelly

Heat butter in large pan. Add cabbage; cook, stirring, until just soft. Add vinegar and jelly; cook, stirring, about 2 minutes or until heated through.

Serves 6.

- Best made just before serving.
- Freeze: Not suitable.
- Microwave: Suitable.

Bowl and plate from Villeroy & Boch

Plates and bowl from Home & Garden on the Mall

WARM THAI-STYLE CABBAGE AND RICE SALAD

1 cup white long-grain rice
2 cups broccoli florets
3 tablespoons peanut oil
2lb Chinese cabbage, chopped
3 cloves garlic, crushed
2 teaspoons grated fresh ginger
1 tablespoon fish sauce
1/4 cup sweet chili sauce
3 tablespoons lime juice
3 tablespoons chopped raw peanuts
3 tablespoons finely chopped fresh cilantro

Cook rice in large pan of boiling water, uncovered, until just tender; drain. Rinse rice under cold water; drain.

Boil, steam or microwave broccoli until just tender; drain.

Heat oil in wok or large pan; stir-fry cabbage, garlic and ginger until cabbage is just soft. Add rice, broccoli and combined sauces, juice and peanuts; cook, stirring, until heated through. Just before serving, stir through cilantro.

Serves 6.

- Best made just before serving.
- Freeze: Not suitable.
- Microwave: Suitable.

OPPOSITE FROM LEFT:
Summertime Cabbage Salad;
Warm Thai-Style Cabbage and Rice Salad.
ABOVE: Braised Red Cabbage.

Cabbage

STIR-FRIED LEAFY CHINESE GREENS

3 tablespoons peanut oil
2lb Chinese cabbage, chopped
12oz baby bok choy, chopped
4 green onions, chopped
1¹/₂ tablespoons soy sauce
3 tablespoons oyster sauce
2 teaspoons sesame oil
1 teaspoon sesame seeds, toasted

Heat peanut oil in wok or large pan; stir-fry cabbage until it begins to soften. Add bok choy, stirring, until just tender. Stir in onions, sauces and sesame oil; stir-fry until well combined and heated through. Serve sprinkled with sesame seeds.

Serves 4 to 6.

■ Best made just before serving.
■ Freeze: Not suitable.
■ Microwave: Not suitable.

CREAMY SPICED CABBAGE

3 tablespoons vegetable oil
1 small onion, sliced
3 cloves garlic, crushed
2 teaspoons grated fresh ginger
2 teaspoons finely chopped fresh lemon grass
1 large onion, sliced
2lb savoy cabbage, chopped
1¹/₂ tablespoons mild curry paste
2 teaspoons all-purpose flour
1 cup coconut milk
1¹/₂ tablespoons lime juice
2 teaspoons fish sauce
¹/₄ teaspoon black onion seeds (kalonji), optional

Heat half the oil in small pan. Add small onion; cook until browned and crisp. Drain on paper towels; reserve.

Heat remaining oil in large pan; cook garlic, ginger, lemon grass and large onion, stirring, until onion is soft. Add cabbage; cook, stirring, about 10 minutes or until soft. Add curry paste and flour; cook, stirring, about 2 minutes or until well combined. Add milk, juice and sauce; simmer, uncovered, about 5 minutes or until mixture thickens slightly. Just before serving, top with reserved fried onion, sprinkle with onion seeds.

Serves 6.

■ Best made just before serving.
■ Freeze: Not suitable.
■ Microwave: Not suitable.

Savoy Cabbage

Common Round Cabbage

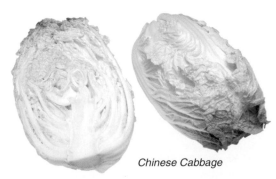

Chinese Cabbage

CABBAGE ROLLS

We used common round cabbage for this recipe.

12 large cabbage leaves
2 cups water
2 medium tomatoes, chopped
3 tablespoons tomato paste
¼ cup lemon juice
4 cloves garlic, crushed

RICE FILLING
**½ cup uncooked white
    long-grain rice**
8oz ground lamb
1½ tablespoons tomato paste
1 teaspoon salt

Remove and discard thick stems from leaves. Boil, steam or microwave leaves until just soft; drain. Rinse leaves under cold water; drain.

Place leaves, vein-side up, on work surface; divide filling among them, placing portion at stem end of each leaf. Roll up firmly, folding in sides to enclose filling. Place rolls close together, seam-side down, in large pan; pour over combined water, tomatoes and paste. Cover rolls with heatproof plate to keep in position during cooking. Bring to boil; simmer, covered, 25 minutes. Remove cover and plate; pour combined juice and garlic over rolls. Simmer, uncovered, about 10 minutes or until sauce thickens.

Rice Filling: Combine ingredients in medium bowl; mix thoroughly.

Makes 12.

■ Best made on day of serving.
■ Storage: Covered, in refrigerator.
■ Freeze: Not suitable.
■ Microwave: Suitable.

Pointed Head Cabbage

COLESLAW WITH A TRIO OF DRESSINGS

Each one of the three recipes on the right makes enough dressing for this amount of coleslaw.

**1lb pointed head
    cabbage, shredded**
1 large carrot, coarsely grated
**1 medium red bell pepper,
    seeded, sliced**
3 green onions, chopped
**¼ cup chopped fresh
    Italian parsley**

Combine all ingredients in large bowl; gently toss with preferred dressing.

Serves 6.

■ Coleslaw best made just before serving. Dressings can be made a day ahead.
■ Storage: Covered, separately, in refrigerator.
■ Freeze: Not suitable.

MAYONNAISE DRESSING

⅓ cup mayonnaise
⅓ cup sour cream
½ teaspoon sugar
1 teaspoon Dijon mustard
1½ tablespoons boiling water
3 tablespoons lime juice

Combine all ingredients in jar or small bowl; mix well.

Makes about 1 cup.

LOW-FAT DRESSING

⅓ cup buttermilk
⅓ cup low-fat yogurt
1½ tablespoons water
3 tablespoons lemon juice

Combine all ingredients in jar or small bowl; mix well.

Makes about 1 cup.

VINAIGRETTE

½ cup olive oil
¼ cup white vinegar
3 tablespoons lemon juice
**1½ tablespoons stone ground
    mustard**
3 cloves garlic, crushed

Combine all ingredients in jar; shake well.

Makes about 1 cup.

*OPPOSITE FROM LEFT:
Stir-Fried Leafy Chinese Greens; Creamy Spiced Cabbage.
LEFT: Cabbage Rolls.
ABOVE, CLOCKWISE FROM TOP:
Vinaigrette; Mayonnaise Dressing;
Low-Fat Dressing; Coleslaw.*

Carrots

Crunching on a cold, crisp carrot is irresistibly satisfying, plus it's a bite full of fiber and betacarotene. A member of the parsley family, the carrot is multi-talented, as good in juices, cakes and dips as it is in soups and stews.

Serving spoon from The Bay Tree Kitchen Shop; bowl and platter from Ware Unique

COOKING METHODS *Cooking times are based on 3 large carrots, peeled, cut into ¹/₂ inch slices.*

- **BOIL** *Add carrots to large pan of boiling water; boil, uncovered, about 7 minutes or until tender. Drain.*

- **STEAM** *Place carrots in steamer basket; cook, covered, over pan of simmering water about 9 minutes or until tender. Drain.*

- **MICROWAVE** *Place carrots and ¹/₄ cup water in large microwave-safe dish. Cover, microwave on HIGH (100%) about 8 minutes or until tender, pausing halfway during cooking time to stir. Drain.*
Tested in an 850-watt oven

MINTED BABY CARROTS WITH GARLIC

2 tablespoons butter
2 cloves garlic, crushed
2 bunches baby
  carrots, trimmed
¹/₂ teaspoon sugar
¹/₄ cup lemon juice
3 tablespoons chopped fresh mint

Heat butter in large shallow pan; cook garlic, stirring, about 2 minutes or until fragrant. Add carrots, sugar and juice; cook, stirring, about 8 minutes or until carrots are tender. Sprinkle with mint.

Serves 4 to 6.

- Best made just before serving.
- Freeze: Not suitable.
- Microwave: Suitable.

MOROCCAN CARROT SALAD

3 large carrots, grated
¹/₂ cup chopped fresh seeded dates
¹/₂ cup slivered almonds, toasted
¹/₄ cup chopped fresh cilantro
¹/₄ cup olive oil
¹/₄ cup white vinegar
2 teaspoons ground cumin
1¹/₂ tablespoons honey

Combine carrots, dates, nuts and cilantro in large bowl; gently toss with combined remaining ingredients.

Serves 4 to 6.

- Can be made 1 hour ahead.
- Storage: Covered, in refrigerator.
- Freeze: Not suitable.

Carrot

Baby or Dutch Carrots

Serving container and mat from The Bay Tree Kitchen Shop

CARROT QUENELLES

4 large carrots, chopped
1 1/2 tablespoons butter
1/3 cup cream
pinch ground nutmeg

Boil, steam or microwave carrots; drain. Blend or process carrots with remaining ingredients until pureed. Using two dessert spoons, form carrot mixture into oval-shaped quenelles.

Serves 4.

■ Best made just before serving.
■ Freeze: Not suitable.

ABOVE LEFT: Moroccan Carrot Salad.
LEFT: Carrot Quenelles.
ABOVE: Minted Baby Carrots with Garlic.

47

HOT AND SWEET CAULIFLOWER

3 tablespoons peanut oil
2 fresh long red chilies, chopped
2 cloves garlic, crushed
1¹/₂ tablespoons finely chopped
**   fresh lemon grass**
1lb cauliflower florets
¹/₄ cup water
1 teaspoon fish sauce
3 tablespoons sweet chili sauce
2 green onions, chopped

Heat oil in medium pan; cook chilis, garlic and lemon grass, stirring, about 2 minutes or until fragrant. Add cauliflower and water; cook, covered, about 5 minutes or until cauliflower is almost tender. Stir in sauces; cook, uncovered, until cauliflower is tender. Just before serving, stir in onions.

Serves 4.
■ Best made just before serving.
■ Freeze: Not suitable.
■ Microwave: Suitable.

CURRIED CAULIFLOWER

1¹/₂ tablespoons ghee or
**   clarified butter**
1 medium onion, chopped
1 clove garlic, crushed
1¹/₂ tablespoons grated fresh ginger
1 teaspoon cumin seeds
1 teaspoon mustard seeds
1 teaspoon ground cumin
1 teaspoon ground coriander
¹/₂ teaspoon ground turmeric
1 cup coconut milk
¹/₄ cup water
1lb cauliflower florets
1 medium tomato, chopped

1¹/₂ tablespoons chopped
**   fresh cilantro**

Heat ghee in medium pan; cook onion garlic and ginger, stirring, until onion is soft. Add seeds and spices; cook stirring frequently, about 5 minutes or until fragrant. Stir in remaining ingredients; simmer, uncovered, about 10 minutes or until cauliflower is just tender and sauce thickened.

Serves 4 to 6.
■ Can be made 3 hours ahead.
■ Storage: Covered, in refrigerator.
■ Freeze: Not suitable.
■ Microwave: Suitable.

Cauliflower

Literally a cabbage cultivated for its tightly furled, edible white florets, cauliflower is another native of North Africa, introduced to the rest of the world by Arab traders. Its gentle, rather bland flavor is an adaptable foil for a great many different treatments.

COOKING METHODS *Cooking times are based on 1lb cauliflower, cut into florets.*

• **BOIL** *Add cauliflower to large pan of boiling water; boil, uncovered, about 4 minutes or until tender. Drain.*

• **STEAM** *Place cauliflower in steamer basket; cook, covered, over pan of simmering water about 4 minutes or until tender. Drain.*

• **MICROWAVE** *Place cauliflower and ¼ cup water in large microwave-safe dish. Cover, microwave on HIGH (100%) about 6 minutes or until tender, pausing halfway during cooking time to stir. Stand 1 minute; drain.*

Tested in an 850-watt oven

CAULIFLOWER GNOCCHI

2 cups milk
¼ teaspoon cayenne
½ cup semolina
1lb cauliflower, chopped
1 teaspoon salt
¾ cup grated parmesan cheese
1 egg, lightly beaten
1½ tablespoons butter, melted
1½ tablespoons chopped
  fresh parsley

Oil 9 x 13in baking dish.

Bring milk and chili powder to boil in medium pan; gradually stir in semolina, cauliflower and salt. Simmer, uncovered, about 12 minutes or until mixture is very thick, stirring frequently. Combine ½ cup of the parmesan with egg; stir into cauliflower mixture. Spread gnocchi mixture into prepared pan; cover, refrigerate 3 hours or until firm.

Using a 2-inch cutter, cut gnocchi mixture into rounds; using spatula, lift rounds onto paper-lined baking tray. Place leftover gnocchi scraps in oiled shallow ovenproof dish; top with overlapping gnocchi, brush with butter, sprinkle with remaining parmesan. Bake, uncovered, in 350ºF oven about 20 minutes or until gnocchi are browned and heated through. Sprinkle with parsley.

Serves 4.

■ Cauliflower Gnocchi mixture can be prepared a day ahead.
■ Storage: Covered, in refrigerator.
■ Freeze: Not suitable.
■ Microwave: Not suitable.

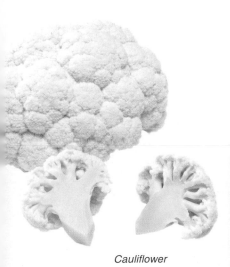

Cauliflower

OPPOSITE FROM LEFT: Hot and Sweet Cauliflower; Curried Cauliflower.
RIGHT. Cauliflower Gnocchi.

Celery

Too often relegated to the back-burner and used only as a base ingredient, celery stands out in the parsley family for its delicately distinct flavor and crisp texture.

GAZPACHO CELERY SALAD

You need a large bunch of celery for this recipe.

1/3 cup red lentils
1 small English cucumber
4oz arugula
1 cup walnuts, toasted
**10 stalks celery, trimmed,
    finely sliced**
12oz pear tomatoes, halved

GAZPACHO DRESSING
1/2 cup tomato juice
1 1/2 tablespoons olive oil
1 1/2 tablespoons chopped fresh dill
1 clove garlic, crushed
1 teaspoon sugar
1 teaspoon red wine vinegar
1/2 teaspoon Tabasco sauce

Rinse lentils under cold water; drain. Cook lentils in small pan of boiling water, uncovered, about 15 minutes or until just tender; drain, cool.

Halve cucumber lengthwise then slice halves finely. Combine lentils and cucumber slices with remaining salad ingredients in large bowl; gently toss with Gazpacho Dressing.
Gazpacho Dressing: Combine all ingredients in jar; shake well.

Serves 6.

■ Salad best made just before serving. Dressing can be made a day ahead.
■ Storage: In jar, in refrigerator.
■ Freeze: Not suitable.

Casserole dish from House

PROSCIUTTO AND TOMATO BAKED CELERY

You need 2 large bunches of celery for this recipe. Remove as much string from stalks of celery as possible.

20 stalks celery
1 1/2 tablespoons olive oil
1 1/2 tablespoons butter
1 medium onion, finely chopped
5 slices prosciutto, chopped
1 clove garlic, crushed
4 large plum tomatoes, chopped
1/3 cup beef stock
1/3 cup grated parmesan cheese

Cut celery into 4-inch lengths. Cook in large pan of boiling water, covered, 6 minutes; drain. Heat oil and butter in large heavy-based pan; cook onion, prosciutto and garlic, stirring, until onion is soft. Add celery, tomatoes and stock; cook, covered, 20 minutes. Transfer mixture to shallow 3-quart ovenproof dish; sprinkle parmesan over the top. Bake, uncovered, in 400ºF oven, about 20 minutes or until browned lightly.

Serves 6 to 8.

■ Best made just before serving.
■ Freeze: Not suitable.
■ Microwave: Celery suitable.

*OPPOSITE: Gazpacho Celery Salad.
ABOVE: Prosciutto and Tomato
Baked Celery.*

Celery

Celery root

Sometimes called knob celery, celery root is a round brown root having a delicious white flesh. The French have long appreciated its flavor but celery root has only just become popular here, thanks to its frequent appearance on bistro menus.

COOKING METHODS *Cooking times are based on 1 large celery root, peeled, cut into 1-inch pieces (approximately 7 cups).*

• **BOIL** *Add celery root to large pan of boiling water; boil, uncovered, about 30 minutes or until tender. Drain.*

• **STEAM** *Place celery root in steamer basket; cook, covered, over pan of simmering water about 40 minutes or until tender. Drain.*

• **MICROWAVE** *Place celery root and 1/4 cup water in large microwave-safe dish. Cover, microwave on HIGH (100%) about 20 minutes or until tender, pausing halfway during cooking time to stir. Stand 2 minutes; drain.*

Tested in an 830-watt oven

CELERY ROOT PUREE

1 large celery root
4 tablespoons butter
1/3 cup buttermilk
1/2 teaspoon ground nutmeg
4 green onions, chopped

Boil, steam or microwave celery root until tender; drain. Mash celery root with butter, buttermilk and nutmeg in large bowl; stir in onions, and salt and pepper to taste.

Serves 4 to 6.

■ Best made just before serving.
■ Freeze: Not suitable.

ROAST CELERY ROOT WITH GARLIC PARSLEY BUTTER

1 large celery root, chopped into 2-inch pieces
1 1/2 tablespoons olive oil
1 medium bulb garlic
4 tablespoons butter
1/4 cup chopped fresh Italian parsley

Toss celery root in oil; place with the unpeeled garlic in large flameproof baking dish. Bake, uncovered, in 350ºF oven about 1 hour or until celery root is tender; remove from pan, keep warm. Cut whole garlic in half horizontally; squeeze pulp into baking dish, discard skin. Add butter and parsley; cook, stirring, until butter melts. Return celery root to dish, toss gently with garlic mixture.

Serves 4 to 6.

■ Best made just before serving.
■ Freeze: Not suitable.
■ Microwave: Not suitable.

CELERY ROOT SALAD WITH HORSERADISH MAYONNAISE

1 medium raw celery root, grated
1 large apple, grated
1 large carrot, grated

HORSERADISH MAYONNAISE
3 egg yolks
1 1/2 tablespoons white wine vinegar
1 1/2 tablespoons chopped fresh sage
2 teaspoons cream style horseradish
1/2 cup olive oil

Combine salad ingredients in large bowl; add Horseradish Mayonnaise, toss gently.

Horseradish Mayonnaise: Blend or process egg yolks, vinegar, sage and horseradish until smooth. With motor operating, gradually pour in oil; process until thick.

Serves 4 to 6.

■ Can be prepared 3 hours ahead.
■ Storage: Covered, in refrigerator.
■ Freeze: Not suitable.

Celery root

CLOCKWISE FROM TOP LEFT: Celery Root Puree; Celery Root Salad with Horseradish Mayonnaise; Roast Celery Root with Garlic Parsley Butter.

Chayote

Known as chokoes, christophene and vegetable pear in various parts of the world, this member of the squash family grows wild from the West Indies to Latin America, where it is regarded as a kitchen staple. The Mexicans, especially, eat it in numerous dishes – from a deep-fried snack with salsa to a dessert stewed with tropical fruits.

Plates and cutlery from House In Newtown

COOKING METHODS *Cooking times are based on 3 large chayotes, peeled, seeded and cut into 1-inch wedges.*

- **BOIL** *Add chayotes to large pan of boiling water; boil, uncovered, about 12 minutes or until tender. Drain.*

- **STEAM** *Place chayotes, in single layer, in steamer basket; cook, covered, over pan of simmering water about 15 minutes or until tender. Drain.*

- **MICROWAVE** *Place chayotes and 1/4 cup water in large microwave-safe bowl. Cover, microwave on HIGH (100%) about 9 minutes or until tender, pausing halfway during cooking time to stir. Stand for 2 minutes; drain.*

Tested in an 830-watt oven

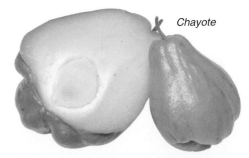

Chayote

CHAYOTE AND POTATO PUREE

2 teaspoons olive oil
1 large leek, finely chopped
1 clove garlic, crushed
3 large chayotes, chopped
6 medium potatoes, chopped
4 tablespoons butter, chopped
2 teaspoons chicken stock base or
** 2 chicken bouillon cubes**
3 tablespoons chopped fresh basil

Heat oil in small pan; cook leek and garlic, stirring, about 5 minutes or until leek is soft.

Boil, steam or microwave chayotes and potatoes, separately, until tender; drain. Blend or process chayotes with the leek mixture until pureed; mash potatoes with butter and chicken base. Combine both mixtures; push through sieve into large bowl, stir in basil.

Serves 4 to 6.

■ Can be made 3 hours ahead.
■ Storage: Covered, in refrigerator.
■ Freeze: Not suitable.

CRUMBED CHAYOTE WEDGES

5 medium chayotes
1/2 cup packaged breadcrumbs
1/4 cup finely grated
** parmesan cheese**
1 clove garlic, finely chopped
2 teaspoons chopped fresh thyme
1 egg, lightly beaten
vegetable oil, for shallow frying

Cut each chayote into 8 wedges. Boil steam or microwave until just tender drain, pat dry.

Combine breadcrumbs, parmesan garlic and thyme in large bowl. Dip wedges in egg, then in breadcrumb mixture. Heat oil in large shallow pan; fry wedges, in batches, until well browned all over. Drain on paper towels.

Makes 40.

■ Best made just before serving.
■ Freeze: Not suitable.

CREAMY BACON CHAYOTES

8 small chayotes
2 teaspoons olive oil
8 bacon slices, finely chopped
2 medium onions, chopped
2 cloves garlic, crushed
⅓ cup cream
2 teaspoons Dijon mustard
**1½ tablespoons chopped
    fresh parsley**

Quarter chayotes lengthwise. Boil, steam or microwave until tender; drain.

Heat oil in large pan; cook bacon, onions and garlic, stirring, until onions are soft. Add chayotes and combined remaining ingredients to pan; stir gently until heated through.

Serves 4 to 6.

■ Best made just before serving.
■ Freeze: Not suitable.

CLOCKWISE FROM TOP LEFT:
Chayote and Potato Puree; Creamy Bacon Chayotes; Crumbed Chayote Wedges.

Corn

Corn, native to the Americas, was introduced by the Indians to the early settlers – no wonder they said Thanks for the Giving. Also known as maize, corn is dried and ground into meal for polenta, into powder for flour or left intact to be popped: kernels of inspiration!

COOKING METHODS *Cooking times are based on 2 medium fresh corn cobs, husk and silk removed and discarded.*

- **BOIL** *Add corn to medium pan of boiling water; boil, uncovered, about 4 minutes or until tender. Drain.*
- **STEAM** *Place corn in steamer basket; cook, covered, over pan of simmering water, about 4 minutes or until tender. Drain.*
- **MICROWAVE** *Place corn and 1 tablespoon water in medium microwave-safe dish. Cover, microwave on HIGH (100%) about 2 minutes or until tender, pausing halfway during cooking time to turn. Drain.*

Tested in an 850-watt oven

Plate from Villeroy & Boch; tiles from Country Floors

CORN, BARLEY AND TOMATO SALAD

3 medium corn cobs
2/3 cup pearl barley, rinsed
2 large green bell peppers, roasted, finely chopped
2 large tomatoes, seeded, sliced
1 medium red onion, thinly sliced
1 baby romaine lettuce
1/3 cup chopped fresh mint

SWEET CHILI DRESSING
1/3 cup olive oil
3 tablespoons sweet chili sauce
3 tablespoons lemon juice
1 teaspoon sugar

Boil, steam or microwave corn until tender; drain. When cool, cut kernels from cobs in strips; discard cobs. Cook barley in medium pan of boiling water, uncovered, about 35 minutes or until tender; drain. Gently toss corn and barley with remaining salad ingredients and Sweet Chili Dressing in large bowl. **Sweet Chili Dressing:** Combine all ingredients in jar; shake well.

Serves 6 to 8.

- Sweet Chili Dressing can be made a day ahead. Salad best made on day of serving.
- Storage: Covered, separately, in refrigerator.
- Freeze: Not suitable.

Corn

BARBECUED CORN WITH LIME BUTTER

6 small corn cobs, husks intact

LIME BUTTER
8 tablespoons butter, softened
2 teaspoons grated lime rind
1 small fresh red chili,
   seeded, chopped
1 1/2 tablespoons chopped
   fresh cilantro

Gently peel husk down corn cob, keeping husk attached at base. Remove as much silk as possible then bring husk back over cob to re-wrap and enclose completely; secure husk at end of cob with string. Cover corn cobs with cold water in large bowl, soak at least 1 hour; drain. Do not allow husk to dry; use as soon as possible after draining.

Cook corn on heated oiled barbecue or griddle pan about 25 minutes or until corn is just tender, turning occasionally. Discard string, serve immediately with Lime Butter.

Lime Butter: Combine all ingredients in small bowl; spoon mixture onto piece of plastic wrap, shape into a 5-inch log. Roll up; refrigerate until firm.

Makes 6.

■ Corn can be soaked up to 8 hours before cooking. Lime Butter can be made a week ahead.
■ Storage: Butter, covered, in refrigerator.
■ Freeze: Butter suitable.

SUCCOTASH

You need approximately 2 medium corn cobs for this recipe. Remove kernels by running a sharp knife down sides of each cob.

4 tablespoons butter
1 small onion, finely chopped
1 bacon slice, finely chopped
2 cups fresh corn kernels
2 small red bell peppers,
   finely chopped
1lb frozen fava beans, cooked
1/4 cup cream

Heat butter in large pan; cook onion, bacon, corn and bell peppers, stirring, about 5 minutes or until corn is tender. Add remaining ingredients, stir until heated through.

Serves 6.

■ Best made on day of serving.
■ Storage: Covered, in refrigerator.
■ Freeze: Not suitable.
■ Microwave: Not suitable.

OPPOSITE: Corn, Barley and Tomato Salad.
RIGHT FROM TOP: Barbecued Corn with Lime Butter; Succotash.

INDONESIAN CUCUMBER SALAD WITH PEANUT DRESSING

2 medium carrots
1 telegraph or English cucumber, sliced
3 cups mung bean sprouts
1¹/₂ tablespoons chopped fresh cilantro

PEANUT DRESSING
¹/₃ cup smooth peanut butter
1 clove garlic, crushed
1 teaspoon sambal oelek [see Glossary]
1¹/₂ tablespoons soy sauce
¹/₂ cup coconut milk
3 tablespoons hot water

Using a vegetable peeler, cut carrots into long thin strips. Gently toss carrot with remaining salad ingredients in large bowl; drizzle with Peanut Dressing.
Peanut Dressing: Combine peanut butter, garlic, sambal oelek, sauce and milk in small bowl. Just before serving, stir in hot water.

Serves 4 to 6.

■ Salad and Peanut Dressing can be prepared 3 hours ahead.
■ Storage: Covered, separately, in refrigerator.
■ Freeze: Not suitable.

LAYERED CUCUMBER SALAD

2 large plum tomatoes
1 lemon cucumber, peeled
1 small red onion, cut into rings

HERB DRESSING
¹/₄ cup olive oil
1¹/₂ tablespoons balsamic vinegar
2 teaspoons chopped fresh marjoram
¹/₂ teaspoon sugar

Cut tomatoes into ¹/₄-inch slices; slice cucumber into ¹/₄-inch rounds. Layer the tomatoes, cucumber and onion in medium bowl; drizzle with Herb Dressing. Cover; refrigerate at least 1 hour before serving.
Herb Dressing: Whisk all ingredients in small bowl until combined.

Serves 4.

■ Salad and Herb Dressing can be prepared 3 hours ahead.
■ Storage: Covered, separately, in refrigerator.
■ Freeze: Not suitable.

LEFT FROM TOP: Indonesian Cucumber Salad with Peanut Dressing;
Layered Cucumber Salad;
Cucumber and Daikon Salad.
OPPOSITE: Sweet Chili Cucumber Salad.

Cucumbers

Thin-skinned yet cool, the multi-talented cucumber can be pungent in a pickle or soothingly sweet in a salad.

SWEET CHILI CUCUMBER SALAD

5 medium English cucumbers
2/3 cup raw peanuts, toasted
4 green onions, chopped
3 tablespoons chopped
**   fresh cilantro**
1 1/2 tablespoons lime juice

SWEET CHILI DRESSING
1 cup white vinegar
1/2 cup sweet chili sauce
1 1/2 tablespoons fish sauce
1 1/2 tablespoons sugar
1 clove garlic, crushed

Halve cucumbers lengthwise; discard seeds, cut diagonally into 1/2-inch slices. Just before serving, gently toss the cucumber, remaining salad ingredients and Sweet Chili Dressing together in medium bowl.
Sweet Chili Dressing: Combine all ingredients in small pan; boil, uncovered, about 10 minutes or until reduced to 3/4 cup. Cool.

Serves 4.

■ Sweet Chili Dressing can be made a day ahead.
■ Storage: Covered, in refrigerator.
■ Freeze: Not suitable.

CUCUMBER AND DAIKON SALAD

3 medium English cucumbers
1/2 daikon [see Radish]
1/4 cup drained pickled
**   pink ginger**
2 green onions, chopped

WASABI DRESSING
3/4 teaspoon wasabi paste
3 tablespoons peanut oil
1 1/2 tablespoons rice vinegar

Using a vegetable peeler, cut cucumbers and daikon into long thin strips. Gently toss cucumber and daikon strips with remaining salad ingredients in large bowl; drizzle with Wasabi Dressing.
Wasabi Dressing: Whisk all ingredients in small bowl until combined.

Serves 4 to 6.

■ Best made just before serving.
■ Freeze: Not suitable.

Placemat and glass bowl from Home & Garden on the Mall

Telegraph Cucumber: An old variety dating back to the days when the telegraph was a new invention. Very long and green with ridges running down its entire length; also called a Continental Cucumber.

Lemon Cucumber: Short, round, plump and pale green in colour. Very fleshy, loaded with soft seeds; its sweet flavor and juiciness make it quite popular.

Green Cucumber: This long, oval-shaped cucumber is the most common.

English Cucumber: Also known as the European or Burpless Cucumber, this variety is long, slender and dark green. It is favored for its juiciness and digestibility.

Eggplants

European folklore has it that eating eggplant skin caused insanity but we prefer the Turkish tale where the sultan fainted with pleasure upon eating a dish of tiny stuffed eggplants... proof of the allure of this seductive vegetable.

BOMBAY EGGPLANTS

8 Japanese eggplants
3 tablespoons peanut oil
2 teaspoons grated fresh ginger
2 cloves garlic, crushed
1 small fresh red chili,
    finely chopped
2 teaspoons ground cumin
2 teaspoons sesame seeds
2 teaspoons coriander seeds
1 teaspoon poppy seeds
3/4 cup coconut milk
1 1/2 tablespoons tamarind pulp
3 tablespoons coconut milk, extra

Quarter eggplants lengthwise but do not cut all the way through at stem end.

Heat oil in wok or large pan; stir-fry ginger, garlic, chili, ground and whole spices 1 minute or until fragrant. Add eggplants; stir-fry 2 minutes. Add milk and tamarind; cook, covered, about 8 minutes or until eggplants are tender, stirring occasionally. Drizzle with extra coconut milk just before serving.

Serves 4 to 6.

■ Best made on day of serving.
■ Storage: Covered, in refrigerator.
■ Freeze: Not suitable.
■ Microwave: Not suitable.

BABA GHANOUSH AND VEGETABLE JULIENNE

1 small English cucumber
1 medium green zucchini
1 medium yellow zucchini
1 medium carrot

BABA GHANOUSH DRESSING
2 Japanese eggplants
1 clove garlic, crushed
3 tablespoons tahini
1 1/2 teaspoons ground cumin
1/2 cup buttermilk
3 tablespoons water
3 tablespoons chopped
    fresh cilantro

Halve cucumber lengthwise; discard seeds. Slice cucumber, zucchini and carrot into paper-thin 4-inch strips; place in medium bowl, drizzle with Baba Ghanoush Dressing.
Baba Ghanoush Dressing: Pierce eggplants all over with fork, place on oven tray; bake, uncovered, in 400ºF oven about 45 minutes or until flesh is soft and skin is blackened. Peel; discard skin, chop flesh roughly. Blend or process

Plate from Villeroy & Boch

60

eggplant, garlic, tahini and cumin until pureed. Add buttermilk and water; process until smooth. Stir in cilantro.

Serves 6.

■ Baba Ghanoush Dressing can be made a day ahead.
■ Storage: Covered, in refrigerator.
■ Freeze: Not suitable.
■ Microwave: Not suitable.

EGGPLANT SALAD CAPRESE

3 small eggplants
salt
2 medium tomatoes, sliced
12oz bocconcini cheese, sliced
¼ cup firmly packed fresh basil

CLASSIC ITALIAN DRESSING
¼ cup olive oil
1 clove garlic, crushed
1 teaspoon stone ground mustard
1 teaspoon sugar
3 tablespoons red wine vinegar

Cut eggplants into ½-inch slices, place on wire racks, sprinkle with salt; stand 30 minutes. Rinse eggplant under cold water; drain on paper towels. Cook eggplant in heated oiled griddle pan until tender and browned on both sides.

Layer eggplant with remaining salad ingredients on serving platter; drizzle with three-quarters of the Classic Italian Dressing. Cover; refrigerate for at least 15 minutes or up to 3 hours. Just before serving, drizzle with the remaining Classic Italian Dressing.

Classic Italian Dressing: Combine all ingredients in a jar; shake well.

Serves 4 to 6.

■ Can be made up to 3 hours before serving.
■ Storage: Covered, in refrigerator.
■ Freeze: Not suitable.

Eggplant

Japanese Eggplant

OPPOSITE: Bombay Eggplants
RIGHT FROM TOP:
Baba Ghanoush and Vegetable Julienne;
Eggplant Salad Caprese.

FENNEL, ASPARAGUS AND ANCHOVY STIR-FRY

1½ tablespoons olive oil
1 large fennel bulb, sliced
8oz asparagus, chopped
½ small red bell pepper, seeded,
    finely chopped
3 tablespoons lemon juice
4 tablespoons butter
3 cloves garlic, crushed
4 anchovy fillets, finely chopped

Heat oil in wok or large pan; stir-fry fennel and asparagus 2 minutes. Add bell pepper, juice and combined butter, garlic and anchovies; stir-fry until the vegetables are just tender.

Serves 4 to 6.

■ Best made just before serving.
■ Freeze: Not suitable.
■ Microwave: Not suitable.

FENNEL AND TOMATO FRITTERS WITH YOGURT

1 small fennel bulb,
    finely chopped
2 large tomatoes,
    seeded, chopped
1 small onion, finely chopped
1 small fresh red chili, seeded,
    finely chopped
2 teaspoons grated lemon rind
¼ cup grated parmesan cheese
1 cup grated cheddar cheese
1 cup all-purpose flour
3 eggs, lightly beaten
vegetable oil, for deep-frying

YOGURT DIPPING SAUCE
¾ cup yogurt
1½ tablespoons lemon juice
1½ tablespoons water
2 teaspoons chopped fresh
    fennel leaves

Combine fennel, tomatoes, onion, chili, rind, cheeses, flour and eggs in medium bowl. Just before serving, deep-fry rounded tablespoons of mixture in hot oil, in batches, until just browned; drain on absorbent paper. Serve warm with Yogurt Dipping Sauce.

Yogurt Dipping Sauce: Combine all ingredients in small bowl; mix well.

Makes about 20.

Serves 4 to 6.

■ Fritters best made just before
    serving. Yogurt Dipping Sauce can
    be made a day ahead.
■ Storage: Covered, in refrigerator.
■ Freeze: Not suitable.

Fennel

Often known by its Italian name of finocchio (and all too often wrongly called anise), fragrant fennel looks a bit like celery, tastes a bit like licorice and, braised with garlic, butter and parmesan, becomes a dish to die for.

COOKING METHODS *Cooking times are based on 2 medium fennel bulbs, stalks and leaves removed, halved lengthwise, bases trimmed to separate halves.*

- **BOIL** *Add fennel pieces to large pan of boiling water; cook, uncovered, about 5 minutes or until tender. Drain.*

- **STEAM** *Place fennel in steamer basket; cook, covered, over pan of simmering water about 5 minutes or until tender. Drain.*

- **MICROWAVE** *Place fennel and 1/4 cup water in large microwave-safe bowl. Cover, microwave on HIGH (100%) about 5 minutes or until tender, pausing halfway during cooking time to turn. Drain.*
Tested in a 750-watt oven

Fennel

FENNEL RIVIERA SALAD

1 large fennel bulb,
   thinly sliced
3 large plum tomatoes,
   halved, sliced
1 small red onion, thinly sliced
11oz can garbanzos, rinsed, drained
1 cup black olives

BASIL VINAIGRETTE
1/4 cup olive oil
3 tablespoons lemon juice
2 cloves garlic, crushed

3 tablespoons shredded
   fresh basil
1 teaspoon ground cumin

Just before serving, gently toss all salad ingredients with Basil Vinaigrette in large bowl.
Basil Vinaigrette: Combine all the ingredients in jar; shake well.
Serves 4.

■ Best made just before serving.
■ Freeze: Not suitable.

OPPOSITE FROM TOP: Fennel, Asparagus and Anchovy Stir-Fry; Fennel and Tomato Fritters with Yogurt. ABOVE: Fennel Riviera Salad.

Salad Tips

- Keep lettuces under refrigeration until shortly before required. Wash lettuces carefully, spin or pat dry then place in a plastic bag, seal tightly and chill at least half an hour to crisp.

- Hand-held mixing wands are good for mixing dressings in a small jar or bowl rather than dirtying a blender or food processor.

THOUSAND ISLAND DRESSING

Prepared mayonnaise can be substituted for our homemade Basic Mayonnaise (see page 69).

1 cup Basic Mayonnaise
1/4 cup tomato ketchup
1 1/2 tablespoons Worcestershire sauce
1/2 teaspoon Tabasco sauce

Place ingredients in small bowl; whisk only until just combined.

Makes about 1 1/2 cups.

- Can be made a day ahead.
- Storage: Covered, in refrigerator.
- Freeze: Not suitable.

BLUE CHEESE DRESSING

Prepared mayonnaise can be substituted for our homemade Basic Mayonnaise (see page 69).

1 cup Basic Mayonnaise
3/4 cup cream
3 tablespoons white wine vinegar
8oz firm blue-vein cheese, crumbled

Blend or process all ingredients until just smooth.

Makes about 2 1/2 cups.

- Can be made a day ahead.
- Storage: Covered, in refrigerator.
- Freeze: Not suitable.

Watercress: Small, dark leaves with a sharp, almost bitter, flavor.

Curly Endive: A cousin of Chicory, with a loose head of fine, spidery, slightly bitter, pale leaves.

Iceberg: Firm, large, round head with crisp, pale-green leaves having a clean, grassy taste.

Lamb's Lettuce: Also known as Lamb's Tongue, Corn Salad or Mâche, it has clusters of tiny, tender, nutty-tasting leaves.

Lettuces

What so many of us think of as lettuce is just the tip of the iceberg – never before have we been so spoiled for choice at the salad bar. With a mix of more than a dozen different varieties of greens readily available, all deservedly worth a fling, it's time to turn over a new leaf.

ITALIAN DRESSING

1/4 cup lemon juice
3 tablespoons white wine vinegar
1 teaspoon sugar
1 clove garlic, crushed
3/4 cup olive oil
1 teaspoon chopped fresh oregano
1 teaspoon chopped fresh thyme
1 teaspoon chopped fresh basil
1 small fresh red chili, coarsely chopped

Blend or process all ingredients until just smooth.

Makes about 1 1/4 cups.

■ Can be made a day ahead.
■ Storage: Covered, in refrigerator.
■ Freeze: Not suitable.

LOW-CALORIE DRESSING

3/4 cup sun-dried tomatoes without oil
3/4 cup hot water
2 green onions, chopped
3/4 cup buttermilk
3 tablespoons roughly chopped fresh Italian parsley
1 clove garlic, crushed
1 1/2 tablespoons lemon juice
1 teaspoon cracked black pepper

Combine tomatoes and water in bowl; let stand 10 minutes. Blend or process undrained tomatoes with remaining ingredients until just smooth.

Makes about 2 cups.

■ Can be made a day ahead.
■ Storage: Covered, in refrigerator.
■ Freeze: Not suitable.

HONEY MUSTARD DRESSING

3/4 cup olive oil
3 tablespoons lemon juice
1 1/2 tablespoons stone ground mustard
1 1/2 tablespoons honey

Blend or process all ingredients until just smooth.

Makes about 1 cup.

■ Can be made a day ahead.
■ Storage: Covered, in refrigerator.
■ Freeze: Not suitable.

CLOCKWISE FROM CENTER TOP: Italian Dressing; Thousand Island Dressing; Blue Cheese Dressing; Honey Mustard Dressing; Low-Calorie Dressing.

Lettuces

Red Oak Leaf: With Green Oak also known as Leaf Lettuce because their delicate leaves can be picked off the plant one at a time.

Green Oak Leaf: Like the Red Oak, loosely packed, large-hearted lettuce with soft, gently frilled leaves and mild flavor.

Mesclun: Often sold as Salad Mix and consisting of an assortment of various edible greens and flowers.

Butter: Also known as Bibb or Boston Lettuce; large, mild-tasting, leaves so sweet and tender they're said to possess the luscious qualities of butter.

Red and Green Coral: Tightly furled, crunchy leaves with a mild, but distinct, taste.

CLOCKWISE FROM TOP: Caesar Dressing; French Dressing; Basic Mayonnaise; Pesto Dressing; Russian Salad Dressing.

PESTO DRESSING

1/2 cup firmly packed
   fresh basil
1/4 cup coarsely grated
   cheese
2 cloves garlic, crushed
3 tablespoons pine nuts, toasted
1 teaspoon cracked black pepper
3/4 cup olive oil
1/4 cup balsamic vinegar

Blend or process all ingredients until just smooth.

Makes about 1 1/2 cups.

■ Can be made a day ahead.
■ Storage: Covered, in refrigerator.
■ Freeze: Not suitable.

RUSSIAN SALAD DRESSING

Prepared mayonnaise can be substituted for our homemade Basic Mayonnaise (see above right).

1 cup Basic Mayonnaise
1/3 cup mild chili sauce
3 tablespoons chopped fresh chives
1/4 cup finely chopped
   pickled gherkin

Blend or process all ingredients until just smooth.

Makes about 1 1/2 cups.

■ Can be made a day ahead.
■ Storage: Covered, in refrigerator.
■ Freeze: Not suitable.

FRENCH DRESSING

1/3 cup olive oil
1/3 cup vegetable oil
1/4 cup white vinegar
1 teaspoon sugar
1 1/2 tablespoons Dijon mustard
1 clove garlic, crushed

Blend or process all ingredients until just smooth.

Makes about 1 cup.

■ Can be made a day ahead.
■ Storage: Covered, in refrigerator.
■ Freeze: Not suitable.

BASIC MAYONNAISE

2 egg yolks
3 tablespoons lemon juice
2 teaspoons Dijon mustard
3/4 cup extra light olive oil

Blend or process yolks, juice and mustard until smooth. With motor operating, gradually pour in oil; process until thick.

Makes about 1 1/4 cups.

■ Can be made a day ahead.
■ Storage: Covered, in refrigerator.
■ Freeze: Not suitable.

CAESAR DRESSING

The way we have cooked the egg here is the process meant when you see a recipe calling for a coddled egg.

1 egg
8 anchovy fillets
2 cloves garlic, crushed
3 tablespoons lemon juice
1/2 cup grated parmesan cheese
1/2 teaspoon cracked black pepper
1/2 cup olive oil
1/3 cup cream

Bring a small pan of water to boil. Add egg, immediately remove pan from heat; cover, allow to stand 3 minutes. Drain; cool egg under running water, peel over small bowl.
   Blend or process egg with remaining ingredients until just smooth and thickened slightly.

Makes about 1 1/2 cups.

■ Can be made 3 hours ahead.
■ Storage: Covered, in refrigerator.
■ Freeze: Not suitable.

Mizuna: Feathery green leaves, edible pale stems; distinctive sharp flavor; from Japan originally, often used in Mesclun mixes.

Mignonette: Deep red or bright-green tinged with red; firm, crisp leaves with a slightly bitter taste. A good, all-purpose salad lettuce.

Romaine and Baby Romaine : Also called Cos, this crisp, elongated lettuce is the classic Caesar Salad green.

Mushrooms

Sometimes called meat for vegetarians, mushrooms are an excellent source of fiber, low in fat and high in vitamin content – one of nature's perfect products. And yummy into the bargain! Treat mushrooms gently, stored in a brown paper bag in the lowest part of your refrigerator, until ready to use them.

Italian Brown:
A mild-tasting variety but more fully flavored than Button, it is good in pasta dishes or cooked whole as it holds its shape. Light to dark brown with an earthy appearance, it is also known as Field or Cremini.

Enoki:
Slender, 4-inch-long body with a tiny head, it is creamy-yellow in color and crisp in texture. Sold in clumps, it has a mild flavor and is good in stir-fries.

WARM MUSHROOM SALAD

8 tablespoons butter
1/4 cup olive oil
1 clove garlic, crushed
8oz oyster mushrooms
8oz Italian brown mushrooms
4oz shiitake mushrooms
4oz mesclun [see Lettuce]
1 1/2 tablespoons lemon juice
1 1/2 tablespoons chopped
   fresh parsley

Heat half the butter and 1 tablespoon of the oil in large pan; cook garlic and mushrooms, stirring, until mushrooms are just tender. Line serving platter with mesclun; place mushroom mixture over leaves. Melt remaining butter; combine with remaining oil, lemon juice and parsley, drizzle over mushrooms.

Serves 4.

◼ Best made just before serving.
◼ Freeze: Not suitable.
◼ Microwave: Suitable.

ENOKI AND BUTTON MUSHROOM SALAD

3 tablespoons olive oil
1 clove garlic, crushed
8oz button mushrooms, halved
4oz enoki mushrooms
1/4 cup macadamia nuts,
   toasted, chopped
4oz arugula
1 cup mung bean sprouts
1/4 cup macadamia oil
3 tablespoons sweet chili sauce
1 1/2 tablespoons chopped
   fresh cilantro
2 teaspoons lime juice

Heat oil in medium pan; cook garlic, stirring, 1 minute. Add button mushrooms; cook, stirring, until browned and just tender. Add enoki mushrooms; cook, stirring, until just wilted.

Gently toss mushrooms with nuts, arugula, sprouts and combined remaining ingredients in large bowl.

Serves 4.

◼ Best made just before serving.
◼ Freeze: Not suitable.
◼ Microwave: Not suitable.

Shiitake: One of the most cultivated mushrooms in the world, it is grey in color and has a rich spicy flavor. Good eaten raw in salads.

Oyster: Also known as Abalone mushroom or Shellfish of the Woods, it has a fluted cap and its pale color ranges from pearly-white or cream, to peach or grey. The soft flesh and delicate flavor make it a delectable treat when eaten raw.

OPPOSITE FROM TOP:
Enoki and Button
Mushroom Salad;
Warm Mushroom Salad.

MUSHROOM RISOTTO

6 cups chicken stock
1/2 cup dry white wine
3 tablespoons olive oil
2 tablespoons butter
1lb button mushrooms, sliced
2 cloves garlic, crushed
2 cups arborio rice [see Glossary]
1/2 cup cream
**1/2 cup coarsely grated
    parmesan cheese**

Bring stock and wine, uncovered, to boil in large pan; cover, reduce heat to low.

Heat oil and butter in large pan; cook mushrooms and garlic, stirring, until mushrooms are tender. Add rice; stir for 1 minute. Add 2/3 cup hot stock mixture to rice mixture; cook, stirring, until liquid is absorbed. Continue adding stock mixture, in batches, stirring until absorbed between each addition. Cooking time, from when the first liquid is added, should be about 35 minutes, or until rice is tender and creamy. Stir in cream; cook, stirring, until cream is absorbed and risotto starts to thicken. Stir in parmesan; serve immediately.

Serves 4-6.

■ Best made just before serving.
■ Freeze: Not suitable.
■ Microwave: Suitable.

MUSHROOM AND LEEK FRITTATA

1 1/2 tablespoons olive oil
1 1/2 tablespoons butter
2 cloves garlic, crushed
1 small leek, thinly sliced
**8oz Italian brown
    mushrooms, sliced**
7oz button mushrooms, sliced
6 eggs
1/2 cup cream
**1/2 cup finely grated
    parmesan cheese**
**1 1/2 tablespoon chopped
    fresh parsley**

Oil and line bottom of 9-inch baking dish with baking paper.

Heat oil and butter in large pan; cook garlic, leek and mushrooms, stirring, until mushrooms are tender. Cool; spread mushroom mixture in prepared pan. Whisk eggs, cream, parmesan and parsley in medium bowl; pour over mushroom mixture in pan. Bake uncovered, in 350°F oven about 45 minutes or until set. Cool in pan; cut into triangles.

Serves 6 to 8.

■ Can be made a day ahead.
■ Storage: Covered, in refrigerator.
■ Freeze: Not suitable.
■ Microwave: Not suitable.

ABOVE FROM TOP: Mushroom and Leek Frittata; Mushroom Risotto.
OPPOSITE: Stir-Fried Mixed Mushrooms.

STIR-FRIED MIXED MUSHROOMS

3 dried shiitake mushrooms
1 1/2 tablespoons peanut oil
2 cloves garlic, crushed
2 teaspoons finely grated
     fresh ginger
3 1/2 oz black fungi
5oz shimeji mushrooms
1lb can straw mushrooms, drained
3oz broccoli florets
1lb choy sum, chopped
2 baby bok choy, chopped
1/4 cup light soy sauce
3 tablespoons sweet chili sauce
1 1/2 tablespoons oyster sauce
1 1/2 tablespoons rice vinegar

Cover dried mushrooms in small bowl with boiling water; let stand 20 minutes. Drain; remove and discard mushroom stems, slice caps thinly.

Heat oil in wok or large pan; stir-fry garlic, ginger and all mushrooms for 1 minute. Add broccoli, choy sum and bok choy; stir-fry 2 minutes. Add combined sauces and vinegar; stir-fry until choy sum and bok choy are just wilted and sauce comes to boil.

Serves 4 to 6.

■ Best made just before serving.
■ Freeze: Not suitable.

*Black Fungus:
Also known as Cloud Ear; originally a tree fungus but now cultivated on wood in steam rooms; should be just briefly cooked.*

Shimeji: Resemble Oyster mushrooms but are grown in clusters on banks of cottonseed hull. Color fades as they mature, ranging from off-white to woody brown; firm texture, mild flavor and succulent.

Mushrooms

MUSHROOM-FILLED BABY BOK CHOY

6 dried shiitake mushrooms
6 baby bok choy
3 tablespoons peanut oil
1lb button mushrooms,
    finely chopped
2 cloves garlic, crushed
2 teaspoons grated fresh ginger
3 tablespoons light soy sauce
1¹/₂ tablespoons oyster sauce
1 teaspoon sesame oil

Cover dried mushrooms in small bow
with boiling water; let stand 20 minutes
Drain; discard mushroom stems, cho
caps finely. Carefully cut each bok cho
lengthwise, no more than about three
quarters of the way through; open eac
bok choy gently, so it forms a V-shape

Heat 1 tablespoon of the oil in wok c
large pan; stir-fry both mushrooms
garlic and ginger until mushrooms ar
soft and almost all liquid is evaporated
Add combined sauces; stir-fry unt
mixture comes to a boil. Remove fror
heat; cool mixture 5 minutes.

Divide filling mixture among bok choy
tie kitchen string [see Glossary] aroun
each bok choy, about 3-inches fror
ends of leaves, to enclose filling. Plac
bok choy, in single layer, in large bam
boo steamer over wok or large pan c
simmering water; steam, covered, abou
5 minutes or until bok choy are tende
and filling is heated through. Drizzle wit
combined heated remaining peanut o
and sesame oil before serving.

Serves 6.

■ Best made just before serving.
■ Freeze: Not suitable.
■ Microwave: Suitable.

BARBECUED MUSHROOMS WITH HERB BUTTER

8 tablespoons butter, melted
1 teaspoon grated lime rind
1¹/₂ tablespoons lime juice
1¹/₂ tablespoons chopped
    fresh parsley
1¹/₂ tablespoons chopped
    fresh basil
6 large flat mushrooms

Combine butter, rind, juice, parsley and
basil in small bowl. Cook mushrooms in
heated oiled griddle pan (or grill or barbecue), brushing with half of the butter
mixture, until mushrooms are just tender
and well browned. Serve accompanied
with remaining butter mixture.

Serves 6.

■ Butter mixture can be made
    a day ahead.
■ Storage: Covered, in refrigerator.
■ Freeze: Not suitable.
■ Microwave: Butter mixture suitable.

ROASTED MUSHROOMS

1lb button mushrooms
1lb Italian brown mushrooms
3 cloves garlic, crushed
¹/₂ cup olive oil
2 teaspoons salt
¹/₂ teaspoon freshly ground
    black pepper

Combine all ingredients in large bowl;
place mixture in single layer in baking
dish. Bake, uncovered, in 400ºF oven
about 20 minutes or until mushrooms
are very soft and browned lightly.

Serves 4 to 6.

■ Best made just before serving.
■ Freeze: Not suitable.
■ Microwave: Not suitable.

MUSHROOM AND ZUCCHINI LASAGNA

medium zucchini
1/2 tablespoons olive oil
medium onion, chopped
cloves garlic, crushed
lb button mushrooms, sliced
cups tomato-based
    pasta sauce
instant lasagna sheets
1/2 cups ricotta cheese
2 cup coarsely grated
    parmesan cheese

Using a vegetable peeler, cut zucchini into thin strips; place on wire rack over tray, sprinkle with salt, let stand 20 minutes. Rinse zucchini under cold water; pat dry with paper towels. Cook zucchini in heated oiled griddle pan until tender and browned on both sides.

Heat oil in large pan; cook onion, garlic and mushrooms, stirring, until mushrooms are soft. Cool; drain, discarding juices from mushrooms.

Spread base of 8-cup ovenproof dish with a quarter of the pasta sauce; top with 2 sheets of the lasagna, mushroom mixture, ricotta, half of the remaining sauce, then zucchini. Cover with remaining lasagna sheets; spread remaining sauce over lasagna, sprinkle with parmesan. Bake, uncovered, in 350°F oven about 45 minutes or until pasta is tender; cover with foil if surface starts to over brown. Let sit 5 minutes before serving.

Serves 8.

■ Best made on day of serving.
■ Storage: Covered, in refrigerator.
■ Freeze: Not suitable.
■ Microwave: Not suitable.

Polka-dot plate from The Bay Tree Kitchen Shop

MUSHROOM RATATOUILLE

1 1/2 tablespoons olive oil
1 large onion, sliced
2 cloves garlic, crushed
1 1/4 lb button mushrooms
2 medium zucchini, sliced
2 Japanese eggplants, sliced
1 small green bell pepper,
    seeded, chopped
14 oz can tomatoes,
    undrained, crushed
1/4 cup tomato paste
1/2 cup chicken stock
1/4 cup dry red wine
1 1/2 tablespoons balsamic vinegar
1 1/2 tablespoons chopped
    fresh oregano

Heat oil in large pan; cook onion and garlic, stirring, until onion is soft. Add mushrooms, zucchini, eggplants and bell pepper; cook, stirring until vegetables are just tender.

Add tomatoes, paste, stock and wine; simmer, uncovered, about 15 minutes or until mixture thickens and vegetables are soft. Just before serving, stir in vinegar and oregano.

Serves 4 to 6.

■ Can be made a day ahead.
■ Storage: Covered, in refrigerator.
■ Freeze: Not suitable.
■ Microwave: Not suitable.

OPPOSITE FROM TOP: Roasted Mushrooms; Barbecued Mushrooms with Herb Butter.
LEFT: Mushroom-Filled Baby Bok Choy.
ABOVE FROM TOP: Mushroom Ratatouille; Mushroom and Zucchini Lasagne.

Okra Tips

■ To avoid its viscous properties, leave the okra whole when cooking them and take care not to slice off the stem too close to the flesh when trimming.

■ Use the smallest, greenest okra available, and scrub away as much of the fuzz on the skin as possible.

OKRA WITH TOMATOES

3 tablespoons olive oil
2 medium onions, thinly sliced
2 cloves garlic, crushed
2 14oz cans tomatoes, undrained, crushed
1lb okra
1 teaspoon sugar
1/4 cup tomato paste
1/4 cup dry red wine
1 1/2 tablespoons chopped fresh oregano

Heat oil in large pan; cook onions and garlic, stirring, until onions are soft. Add all remaining ingredients; simmer uncovered, about 30 minutes or until okra is tender.

Serves 4 to 6.

■ Can be made a day ahead.
■ Storage: Covered, in refrigerator.
■ Freeze: Not suitable.
■ Microwave: Not suitable.

CLOCKWISE FROM TOP: Okra with Tomatoes; Crunchy Cajun Okra with Chili Mayonnaise; Masala Okra.

Okra

Okra is one of those flavorsome yet misunderstood vegetables which, when handled properly, rewards the cook immensely. A native of Africa, okra was transported, along with the slaves, to the Deep South where it became a staple ingredient in Creole cooking, particularly in many a delicious gumbo.

All bowls and tray from Home & Garden on the Mall

Okra

MASALA OKRA

3 tablespoons ghee or
   clarified butter
2 medium onions, thinly sliced
2 teaspoons grated fresh ginger
2 cloves garlic, crushed
1 teaspoon black mustard seeds
1 small fresh red chili, thinly sliced
1 teaspoon garam masala
2 teaspoons ground cumin
1lb okra
1 cup water
1/2 cup coconut milk
11/2 tablespoons chopped
   fresh cilantro

Heat ghee in large pan; cook onions, ginger and garlic, stirring, until onions are soft. Add seeds, chili and spices; cook, stirring, until fragrant. Add okra and water; simmer, uncovered, about 30 minutes or until okra is soft and liquid evaporated. Add coconut milk and cilantro; stir until heated through.

Serves 4 to 6.

■ Can be made a day ahead.
■ Storage: Covered, in refrigerator.
■ Freeze: Not suitable.
■ Microwave: Not suitable.

CRUNCHY CAJUN OKRA WITH CHILI MAYONNAISE

1lb okra
all-purpose flour
3 eggs, lightly beaten
1 cup cornmeal
3 tablespoons Cajun seasoning
   [see Glossary]
2 teaspoons seasoned salt
vegetable oil, for deep-frying

CHILI MAYONNAISE
1 egg
11/2 tablespoons lime juice
1 clove garlic, crushed
1 cup light olive oil
11/2 tablespoons chopped
   fresh cilantro
11/2 tablespoons sambal oelek
   [see Glossary]

Coat okra with flour, shake away excess; dip into eggs, then coat with combined polenta, seasoning and salt. Deep-fry okra in hot oil, in batches, until golden brown and tender (watch that oil is not so hot that okra overbrowns before it is cooked through). Serve with Chili Mayonnaise.

Chili Mayonnaise: Blend or process egg, juice and garlic until smooth. With motor operating, gradually pour in oil; process until thick. Stir in cilantro and sambal oelek.

Serves 4 to 6.

■ Chili Mayonnaise can be made
  a day ahead.
■ Storage: Covered, in refrigerator.
■ Freeze: Not suitable.
■ Microwave: Not suitable.

Onions

Members of the onion family are usually regarded as the workhorses of the kitchen, basic rather than main ingredients... what a waste of fabulous flavors, amazing versatility and endless possibilities. Knowing your onions means using them, cooked and raw, as heroes in your culinary adventures so that you can create a mouth watering collection of truly epic proportions.

Chives

Garlic

Red Onion

Yellow Onion

White Onion

Green Onion

Spring Onion

Shallots

Pickling Onions

Leek

Garlic Chives

DYNAMITE FRIED ONION RINGS

4 medium yellow onions
1/2 cup all-purpose flour
1/2 cup cornstarch
3 tablespoons Cajun seasoning
   [see Glossary]
1/4 cup water
1 egg
vegetable oil, for deep-frying
1 cup sour cream
1/4 cup hot chili sauce
2 tablespoons chopped
   fresh cilantro
11/2 tablespoons lime juice
1 clove garlic, crushed
2 teaspoons grated lime rind

Cut onions into 1/2-inch slices; separate into rings. Add onion rings to medium pan of boiling water; when water re-boils, drain immediately. Pat onion rings dry with paper towels.

Combine flour, cornstarch and seasoning in medium bowl; whisk in combined water and egg until smooth. Dip rings, a few at a time, into batter; deep-fry rings in hot oil, in batches, until crisp and browned lightly. Drain on paper towels. Serve onion rings with dipping sauce made of combined remaining ingredients.

Serves 4 to 6.

■ Onions must be made just before serving. Dipping sauce can be made a day ahead.
■ Storage: Sauce, covered, in refrigerator.
■ Freeze: Not suitable.
■ Microwave: Not suitable.

MEXICAN-STYLE BARBECUED ONIONS

4 medium red onions
1oz packet taco seasoning
1 large avocado
2 teaspoons lemon juice
1/2 small onion, finely chopped
few drops Tabasco sauce
1/3 cup sour cream
11/2 tablespoons chopped
   fresh cilantro

Cut onions into 1/2-inch slices; coat slices with seasoning. Cook slices, in batches, in a heated oiled griddle pan (or grill or barbecue) until browned on both sides and tender. Meanwhile, place avocado in medium bowl, mash roughly with a fork; stir in lemon juice, onion and Tabasco.

Serve onions topped with avocado mixture, sour cream and cilantro.

Serves 4 to 6.

■ Best made just before serving.
■ Freeze: Not suitable.
■ Microwave: Not suitable.

*OPPOSITE FROM LEFT:
Mexican-Style Barbecued Onions;
Dynamite Fried Onion Rings.*

SWEET AND SOUR LEEKS

3 large leeks
3 tablespoons vegetable oil
3 tablespoons butter
½ cup lemon juice
3 tablespoons sugar

Halve each leek lengthwise; halve each piece crosswise. Secure each piece with a toothpick.

Heat oil and butter in large shallow pan; cook leeks, over low heat, until tender and browned lightly, turning occasionally. Remove leeks from pan; keep warm. Add juice and sugar to same pan, bring to boil; simmer, stirring, about 5 minutes or until sauce reduces to a syrupy consistency. Pour sauce over leeks.

Serves 4.

■ Best made just before serving.
■ Freeze: Not suitable.
■ Microwave: Not suitable.

Platter and cover from Corso De' Fiori

ONIONS AND TOMATOES PROVENÇALE

12 small yellow onions, halved
1 medium bulb garlic, unpeeled
4 large plum tomatoes, quartered
3 sprigs fresh rosemary
3 sprigs fresh thyme
1/3 cup olive oil
1/4 cup red wine vinegar
1 1/2 tablespoons brown sugar

Combine onions, garlic, tomatoes, herbs and half the oil in large bowl; spread mixture in flameproof baking dish. Bake, uncovered, in 325ºF oven about 2 hours or until vegetables are tender, turning twice during cooking time. Remove onions and tomatoes to serving dish.

Squeeze pulp from 5 of the garlic cloves into same baking dish; discard remaining garlic and herbs. Add remaining oil, vinegar and sugar to same dish; cook, stirring, about 10 minutes or until sauce reduces slightly. Pour sauce over onions and tomatoes.

Serves 4 to 6.

■ Best made just before serving.
■ Freeze: Not suitable.
■ Microwave: Not suitable.

WHITE BEAN AND GARLIC PUREE

1 cup dried cannellini beans
4 large cloves garlic,
  coarsely chopped
3 tablespoons white vinegar
1 1/2 tablespoons lemon juice
1/3 cup olive oil

Cover beans in medium bowl with cold water; soak overnight.

Drain beans, transfer to medium pan of cold water. Bring to boil; simmer, covered, about 2 hours or until beans are tender. Drain. Blend or process beans, garlic, vinegar and juice until smooth. With motor operating, gradually pour in oil; process until pureed.

Serves 4 to 6.

■ Can be made a day ahead.
■ Storage: Covered, in refrigerator.
■ Freeze: Not suitable.
■ Microwave: Not suitable.

CARAMELIZED MIXED ONIONS

1 large bulb garlic
4 tablespoons butter
3 tablespoons olive oil
24 shallots
6 spring onions, halved
10 green onions, halved
1 1/2 tablespoons balsamic vinegar

Separate garlic bulb into cloves; peel cloves. Heat butter and oil in large pan; cook garlic, shallots and spring onions about 45 minutes, stirring, until tender and browned. Add green onions; cook, stirring, until just tender. Drizzle with vinegar; serve immediately.

Serves 4 to 6.

■ Best made just before serving.
■ Freeze: Not suitable.
■ Microwave: Not suitable.

OPPOSITE ABOVE: Sweet and Sour Leeks.
OPPOSITE FROM LEFT: Onions and Tomatoes Provençale; White Bean and Garlic Puree.
ABOVE: Caramelized Mixed Onions.

83

Parsnips

This simple white root vegetable undergoes a change in flavor with the first sign of cold weather when its starch is converted to sugar, resulting in the distinctive sweet earthiness that marries so well with the Sunday roast.

COOKING METHODS

Cooking times are based on 4 medium parsnips, peeled, roughly chopped.

- **BOIL** *Add parsnips to large pan of boiling water; boil, uncovered, about 8 minutes or until tender. Drain.*

- **STEAM** *Place parsnips in steamer basket; cook, covered, over pan of simmering water about 8 minutes or until tender. Drain.*

- **MICROWAVE** *Place parsnips and 2 tablespoons water in large microwave-safe dish. Cover, microwave on HIGH (100%) about 6 minutes or until tender, pausing halfway during cooking time to turn. Drain.*

Tested in an 850-watt oven

OVEN-BAKED PARSNIP CHIPS

6 medium parsnips
1 teaspoon salt
1/3 cup olive oil
2 sprigs fresh rosemary
6 large cloves garlic, unpeeled
1/4 teaspoon sweet paprika

Using a crinkle cutter or sharp knife, cut parsnips into thick slices; cut slices into 2 1/2-inch-long chips.

Toss chips with combined remaining ingredients in large bowl; place coated chips in single layer in baking dish. Bake, uncovered, in 400ºF oven about 45 minutes or until chips are browned and crisp, turning occasionally.

Serves 4.

■ Best made just before serving.
■ Freeze: Not suitable.
■ Microwave: Not suitable.

Parsnip

PARSNIP AND CARROT RIBBONS

2 large parsnips
2 large carrots
vegetable oil, for deep-frying

Using a vegetable peeler, peel thin strips from parsnips and carrots. Heat oil in large pan; deep-fry parsnip and carrot strips, separately, in batches, until browned and crisp. Drain on paper towels; serve immediately.

Serves 4.

■ Must be made just before serving.
■ Freeze: Not suitable.
■ Microwave: Not suitable.

PARSNIP, SWEET POTATO AND SPINACH PARFAIT

6 medium parsnips, chopped
2 medium orange sweet potatoes, chopped
1 cup hot buttermilk
3 tablespoons butter, melted
½ cup coarsely grated parmesan cheese
1 small onion, chopped
3 bacon slices, chopped
8oz baby spinach leaves, shredded

Boil, steam or microwave parsnips and sweet potatoes, separately, until tender; drain. Blend or process parsnips until pureed; push puree through fine sieve into large bowl. Stir half the buttermilk, butter and cheese into puree; cover to keep warm.

Puree sweet potato; push puree through fine sieve into separate large bowl. Stir remaining buttermilk, butter and cheese into sweet potato puree; cover to keep warm.

Cook onion and bacon in large pan until bacon is crisp; stir in spinach, cook until just wilted.

Swirl parsnip and sweet potato purees and spinach mixture, in layers, in a serving dish.

Serves 4 to 6.

■ Best made just before serving.
■ Freeze: Not suitable.

OPPOSITE FROM TOP: Parsnip, Sweet Potato and Spinach Parfait; Oven-Baked Parsnip Chips.
ABOVE: Parsnip and Carrot Ribbons.

Green peas

COOKING METHODS *Cooking times are based on 1lb fresh green peas, shelled (approximately 1¼ cups).*

- **BOIL** *Add green peas to small pan of boiling water; boil, uncovered, about 5 minutes or until tender. Drain.*

- **STEAM** *Place green peas in steamer basket; cook, covered, over pan of simmering water about 3 minutes or until tender. Drain.*

- **MICROWAVE** *Place green peas and 1 tablespoon water in large microwave-safe dish. Cover, microwave on HIGH (100%) about 3 minutes or until tender, pausing halfway during cooking time to stir. Drain.*

Tested in an 830-watt oven

GREEN PEA PUREE WITH POTATOES

You need approximately 5lb of unshelled green peas (about 2lb shelled peas) for this recipe. Buy medium-sized, similar-shaped fingerlings to make the finished dish appealing in appearance.

**18 fingerling potatoes
  [see Potatoes]
6 cups shelled green peas
¼ cup finely grated
  parmesan cheese
⅓ cup cream
1 teaspoon cracked black pepper
¼ cup parmesan cheese, shaved**

Boil, steam or microwave potatoes and peas, separately, until just tender; drain.

 Blend or process peas with grated parmesan, cream and pepper until pureed. Place 3 potatoes on individual serving plates; press each with potato masher to break skin, top with pea puree and shaved parmesan.

Serves 6.

■ Best made just before serving.
■ Freeze: Not suitable.

RIGHT: Green Pea Puree with potatoes.
OPPOSITE FROM TOP LEFT:
Quartet of Peas in Minted Cilantro Butter;
Sugar Snap Peas with Toasted Pecans.

Snow Pea
Sprouts

Green Peas

Peas

The pea is believed to have been cultivated in prehistory, and its seeds were found in ancient Egyptian tombs. It has stood the test of time because it tastes of spring, and its tender pods, delicate tendrils and white flowers make it visually appealing. And besides, pea stands for perfect.

Sugar snap and Snow peas

COOKING METHODS *Cooking times are based on 8oz sugar snap peas or snow peas, ends trimmed, strings removed.*

- **BOIL** *Add peas to small pan of boiling water; boil, uncovered, about 2 minutes or until tender. Drain.*

- **STEAM** *Place peas in steamer basket; cook, covered, over pan of simmering water about 3 minutes or until tender. Drain.*

- **MICROWAVE** *Place peas and 2 teaspoons water in large microwave-safe dish. Cover, microwave on HIGH (100%) about 2 minutes or until tender, pausing halfway during cooking time to stir. Drain.*

Tested in an 830-watt oven

SUGAR SNAP PEAS WITH TOASTED PECANS

4 tablespoons butter
3 tablespoons lemon juice
1½ tablespoons brown sugar
1½ tablespoons cracked black pepper
¼ cup chopped pecans, toasted
1¼lb sugar snap peas

Heat butter in medium pan; cook remaining ingredients about 3 minutes or until peas are just tender, stirring frequently.

Serves 4 to 6.

■ Best made just before serving.
■ Freeze: Not suitable.
■ Microwave: Suitable.

Sugar Snap Peas

Snow Peas

QUARTET OF PEAS IN MINTED CILANTRO BUTTER

1¼ cups shelled green peas
7oz snow peas
7oz sugar snap peas
2oz snow pea sprouts

MINTED CILANTRO BUTTER
2 teaspoons vegetable oil
1 medium onion, chopped
1 clove garlic, crushed

⅓ cup coarsely chopped fresh mint
⅓ cup coarsely chopped fresh cilantro
4 tablespoons butter, softened

Boil, steam or microwave shelled green peas, snow peas and sugar snap peas, separately, until just tender; drain. Combine peas with sprouts and Minted Cilantro Butter; serve immediately.

Minted Cilantro Butter: Heat oil in small pan; cook onion and garlic, stirring, until onion is soft. Cool. Blend or process onion mixture with remaining ingredients until pureed.

Serves 4 to 6.

■ Best made just before serving.
■ Freeze: Minted Cilantro Butter suitable.

*King Edward:
Slightly plump
and rosy;
great mashed.*

*Tiny New Potatoes: Also
known as Chats. Not a
variety but an early
harvest with a thin,
pale skin that's easily
rubbed off.
Good
steamed,
and eaten
hot or cold
in salads.*

*Fingerling: Small
and finger-shaped;
it has a nutty flavor
and is great baked
and in salads.*

*Desiree: Oval-
shaped with a
smooth, pink
skin and
waxy, yellow
flesh. Good
both boiled
and roasted, it's
also one of the
best for mashing.*

*Pink Fir Apple:
Elongated with a
rosy skin and waxy
flesh; is good
boiled, baked
and in salads.*

Potatoes

*One potato, two potato, three potato, four... but who
would have dreamed that the "more" we counted up to
would one day exceed the 30 varieties now grown in this
country? Fried, mashed, roasted, boiled or baked, the
potato is the most widely cooked of all vegetables, tastes
great, is virtually fat-free and is a good source of fiber –
no wonder its absence could start a revolution.*

COOKING METHODS *Cooking
times are based on 5 medium potatoes,
peeled, quartered.*

• **BOIL** *Add potatoes to large pan of
boiling water; boil, uncovered, about
15 minutes or until tender. Drain.*

• **STEAM** *Place potatoes in steamer
basket; cook, covered, over pan of
simmering water about 20 minutes or
until tender. Drain.*

• **MICROWAVE** *Place potatoes and
2 tablespoons water in large
microwave-safe dish. Cover, microwave
on HIGH (100%) about 10 minutes or
until tender, pausing halfway during
cooking time to stir. Drain.*

Tested in an 850-watt oven

NICE 'N' SPICY WEDGES

5 large Idaho potatoes
1½ tablespoons cornstarch
**5 tablespoons ghee or
    clarified butter**
1 medium onion, finely chopped
2 cloves garlic, crushed
2 teaspoons grated fresh ginger
1 teaspoon brown mustard seeds
1 teaspoon cumin seeds
2 teaspoons garam masala
½ teaspoon cayenne
**1 teaspoon sumac [see Glossary]
    or taramind concentrate**
1 teaspoon salt
¼ cup lemon juice
**3 tablespoons finely chopped
    fresh cilantro**

Halve potatoes lengthways; cut each half
into 3 wedges. Boil, steam or microwave
potatoes until almost tender; drain. When
cool, toss potatoes in cornstarch.

Heat about 1 tablespoon of the ghee
in medium pan; cook onion, garlic and
ginger, stirring, until onion is soft. Add
seeds, garam masala and chili; cook,
stirring, until fragrant. Remove from
heat, stir in sumac or Stamarind and salt.

Heat half remaining ghee in large pan;
cook half the potatoes about 5 minutes
or until browned and crisp all sides.
Remove from pan, keep warm; repeat
with remaining ghee and potatoes.

Toss all potatoes together in same
pan with reserved spice mixture, juice
and cilantro.

Serves 6.

■ Best made just before serving.
■ Freeze: Not suitable.

*Pontiac: Large and round, it has a
red skin marked with deep eyes,
and the flesh is white. Good
grated, boiled and baked.*

*eruvian: Small and elongated
with purple skin and flesh;
sweet and floury, best used
fried for chips.*

*Idaho: Also
known as Russet
Burbank; ruddy
color, fabulous
baked and fried.*

OPPOSITE: Nice 'N' Spicy Wedges.

ROASTED POTATO SALAD WITH BASIL MAYONNAISE

2lb tiny new potatoes, unpeeled
3 tablespoons olive oil
7oz button mushrooms, sliced
1/3 cup sun-dried tomatoes in oil, drained, sliced
1/3 cup pine nuts, toasted
3 tablespoons shredded fresh basil

BASIL MAYONNAISE
3 egg yolks
3 cloves garlic, coarsely chopped
1 1/2 tablespoons Dijon mustard
1/4 cup white wine vinegar
3/4 cup olive oil
1/3 cup firmly packed fresh basil, shredded
1/4 teaspoon freshly ground black pepper

Place potatoes in baking dish, drizzle with half the oil; bake, uncovered, in 350ºF oven, about 45 minutes or until potatoes are tender.

Meanwhile, heat remaining oil in large pan; cook mushrooms, stirring, about 4 minutes or until browned. Gently toss warm potatoes and mushrooms with tomatoes, pine nuts, basil and Basil Mayonnaise in large bowl.

Basil Mayonnaise: Blend or process egg yolks, garlic, mustard and vinegar until smooth. With motor operating, gradually pour in oil; process until thick. Add basil and pepper; process briefly. Makes about 2 cups.

Serves 4 to 6.

■ Roasted Potato Salad best made just before serving. Mayonnaise can be made a day ahead.
■ Storage: Covered, in refrigerator.
■ Freeze: Not suitable.
■ Microwave: Not suitable.

POTATO FATTOUSH

Fattoush, the Syrian and Lebanese deliciously healthy salad that cleverly uses yesterday's bread as a main ingredient, is even more substantial with the addition of potatoes.

3lb desiree potatoes, unpeeled
2 large rounds pita bread
2 cups firmly packed fresh Italian parsley, coarsely chopped
1 medium onion, thinly sliced
4 large plum tomatoes, chopped
2 medium English cucumbers, thinly sliced
1/4 cup fresh mint, coarsely chopped
2/3 cup light olive oil
1/2 cup lemon juice
1/2 teaspoon freshly ground black pepper

Pink-Eye: Small with off-white skin and deep purple eyes; good steamed, boiled and baked.

Spunta: Large, long, yellow-fleshed and floury; great mashed and fried.

Yukon Gold: Oval-shaped with a creamy skin and yellow flesh; great baked and fried, good in salads.

Creamers: White skin, oval-shaped; good fried, mashed and baked.

Bowls from Prima Cosa; tray from Lime Bay

TRI-FRIES WITH CHILI SALT

1 medium orange sweet potato, unpeeled
1 medium white sweet potato, unpeeled
2 medium new potatoes, unpeeled vegetable oil, for deep-frying
1½ teaspoons salt
¼ teaspoon cayenne
¼ teaspoon freshly cracked black pepper

Scrub all potatoes; pat dry. Using a V-slicer [see Glossary], slice potatoes very thinly. Heat oil in large pan; deep-fry slices, in batches, until golden brown and crisp, drain on paper towels. Sprinkle hot fries with combined remaining ingredients and serve fries immediately.

Serves 6.

■ Must be made just before serving.
■ Freeze: Not suitable.
■ Microwave: Not suitable.

Boil, steam or microwave potatoes until just tender; drain. When cool enough to handle, peel; cut into 1-inch pieces.

Split each pita in half; toast in 400°F oven until crisp. Break pita halves into small, even-size pieces. Combine pita pieces with potatoes, parsley, onion, tomatoes and cucumbers in large bowl. Just before serving, pour combined remaining ingredients over fattoush mixture; toss gently to combine.

Serves 6 to 8.

■ Best made just before serving.
■ Freeze: Not suitable.

ABOVE FROM LEFT: Roasted Potato Salad with Basil Mayonnaise; Potato Fattoush.
RIGHT: Tri-Fries with Chili Salt.

Bowl from House in Newtown

ROASTED TINY NEW POTATOES WITH AIOLI

1³/₄lb tiny new potatoes, unpeeled
3 tablespoons olive oil
1 large bulb garlic, unpeeled
3 tablespoons lemon juice
2 egg yolks
³/₄ cup olive oil, extra
3 tablespoons shredded fresh
   Italian parsley

Combine potatoes and oil in baking dish; wrap whole garlic bulb in double thickness of foil. Bake potatoes and garlic, uncovered, in 350°F oven about 45 minutes or until potatoes and garlic are tender. Turn potatoes once, halfway during cooking time.

Separate garlic cloves. Remove and discard skins from 8 garlic cloves; keep remaining garlic and potatoes warm.

Blend or process peeled garlic, juice and egg yolks until pureed. With motor operating, gradually pour in extra oil; process until aïoli thickens. Stir parsley into aïoli; serve with potatoes and remaining unpeeled garlic cloves.

Serves 6.

■ Best made just before serving.
■ Freeze: Not suitable.
■ Microwave: Not suitable.

PESTO MASHED POTATOES

1¹/₂ tablespoons shredded
   fresh basil
3 tablespoons pine nuts, toasted
3 cloves garlic, coarsely chopped
¹/₄ cup sun-dried tomatoes in oil,
   drained, coarsely chopped
¹/₄ cup coarsely grated
   parmesan cheese
3 tablespoons lemon juice
¹/₄ cup olive oil
3lb creamer potatoes, peeled,
   coarsely chopped
6 tablespoons butter
¹/₂ cup hot cream
¹/₃ cup hot milk

Blend or process basil, pine nuts, garlic, tomatoes, cheese and juice until pureed. With motor operating, gradually pour in oil; process until pesto is smooth.

Just before serving, boil, steam or microwave potatoes until tender; drain. Transfer warm potatoes to large bowl; mash with combined butter, cream and milk until smooth. Swirl pesto through potato mixture.

Serves 6 to 8.

■ Pesto can be made a day ahead.
■ Storage: Covered, in refrigerator.
■ Freeze: Not suitable.

Strainer, bowl and chopping board from Accoutrement; salad servers from House In Newtown

BOMBAY POTATO MASALA

3lb spunta potatoes
1¹/₂ tablespoons butter
1 large onion, sliced
3 cloves garlic, crushed
1 teaspoon yellow mustard seeds
1 tablespoon garam masala
2 teaspoons ground coriander
2 teaspoons ground cumin
¹/₂ teaspoon chili powder
¹/₄ teaspoon ground turmeric
14oz can tomatoes,
   undrained, crushed

Cut potatoes into wedges. Boil, steam or microwave potato wedges until just tender; drain.

Heat butter in large pan; cook onion and garlic, stirring, until onion is soft. Add seeds and spices; cook, stirring, until fragrant. Stir in tomatoes; cook, stirring, 2 minutes or until sauce thickens slightly. Add potatoes; gently stir until heated through.

Serves 6 to 8.

■ Best made just before serving.
■ Freeze: Not suitable.

*LEFT: Bombay Potato Masala.
OPPOSITE FROM TOP: Roasted
Tiny New Potatoes with Aïoli;
Pesto Mashed Potatoes.*

Potatoes

GRANDMA GRACE'S POTATO SALAD

3lb fingerling potatoes, unpeeled
6 hard-boiled eggs, chopped
1 medium red onion, finely chopped
6 green onions, finely chopped
1 cup finely chopped
   drained gherkins
3 tablespoons chopped
   fresh parsley
1 cup mayonnaise
1/4 cup lemon juice
3 tablespoons white vinegar
3 cloves garlic, finely chopped

Boil, steam or microwave potatoes until tender; drain. When cool enough to handle, peel; cut into 1-inch pieces. Gently toss potatoes with eggs, onions, gherkins, parsley and combined remaining ingredients in large bowl.

Serves 6 to 8.

■ Can be made 3 hours ahead.
■ Storage: Covered, in refrigerator.
■ Freeze: Not suitable.

WARM POTATO SALAD

10 shallots, finely chopped
3 tablespoons extra virgin olive oil
2 bacon slices, finely chopped
1 3/4 lb tiny new potatoes,
   unpeeled, sliced
3 tablespoons balsamic vinegar
3 tablespoons chopped
   fresh parsley

Combine shallots and oil in small bowl; stand 30 minutes.

Meanwhile, cook bacon in small oiled pan until crisp; drain bacon on paper towels. Boil, steam or microwave potatoes until just tender; drain. Combine potatoes in large bowl with undrained shallots, bacon and vinegar; cover, stand about 10 minutes. Just before serving, stir in parsley.

Serves 4.

■ Best made just before serving.
■ Freeze: Not suitable.

RIGHT FROM TOP: Grandma Grace's Potato Salad; Warm Potato Salad.
OPPOSITE: Crispy Potato Skins with Mashed Potatoes and Chili Jam.

Glass bowl from Albi Imports

CRISPY POTATO SKINS WITH MASHED POTATOES AND CHILI JAM

6 medium creamer potatoes, unpeeled
1/2 cup hot milk
4 tablespoons butter, melted
vegetable oil, for deep-frying

CHILI JAM
2 medium tomatoes, chopped
1 1/2 tablespoons Worcestershire sauce
3 tablespoons water
3 tablespoons brown sugar
1/4 cup sweet chili sauce
1 1/2 tablespoons chopped fresh cilantro

Mash remaining potato flesh with combined milk and butter until smooth; cover to keep warm.

Heat oil in large pan; deep-fry potato-skin strips, in batches, in hot oil until browned and crisp. Drain on paper towels. Serve immediately with mashed potatoes and Chili Jam.

Chili Jam: Combine all ingredients in medium pan; stir over low heat until sugar dissolves. Bring to boil; simmer, uncovered, about 15 minutes or until jam thickens and is reduced to about 2/3 cup. Remove from heat; cool slightly, stir in cilantro.

Serves 6.

■ Chili Jam can be made 2 days ahead.
■ Storage: Covered, in refrigerator.
■ Freeze: Not suitable.

Plate and bowls from Accoutrement

Scrub potatoes; boil, steam or microwave until tender. Drain.
When cool enough to handle, cut away 5 strips from each potato, cutting about 1/2-inch into the flesh; reserve strips.

95

Pumpkins
and winter squash

Belonging to the same gourd family as zucchini and chayotes, the pumpkin was domesticated by natives of the New World, and introduced to Europe by the colonists. It has become a symbol of the fall harvest and of course the indispensable source of jack-o-lanterns every Halloween!

Tiles from Country Floors

COOKING METHODS *Cooking times are based on 1lb pumpkin, peeled, seeded, chopped.*

- **BOIL** *Add pumpkin to large pan of boiling water; boil, uncovered, about 8 minutes or until tender. Drain.*

- **STEAM** *Place pumpkin in steamer basket; cook, covered, over pan of simmering water about 20 minutes or until tender. Drain.*

- **MICROWAVE** *Place pumpkin and 1 tablespoon water in large microwave-safe dish. Cover, microwave on HIGH (100%) about 5 minutes or until tender, pausing halfway during cooking time to stir. Drain.*

Tested in an 830-watt oven

Butternut Squash: Small and pear-shaped with bright-orange flesh. Has a sweet, nutty flavor complementary to many vegetable dishes.

ROASTED SQUASH PUREE

4lb butternut squash, chopped
3 tablespoons olive oil
¼ cup buttermilk
½ cup finely grated
    parmesan cheese
4 tablespoons butter, chopped
¼ teaspoon ground nutmeg

Combine squash and oil in baking dish; bake, uncovered, in 425ºF oven about 1 hour or until squash is tender and browned lightly.

Transfer squash to large bowl. Working quickly, mash squash then push through fine sieve back into same bowl. Stir in remaining ingredients and serve immediately.

Serves 4 to 6.

■ Best made just before serving.
■ Freeze: Not suitable.
■ Microwave: Not suitable.

Bowl from Gemp; tiles from Country Floors

PUMPKIN CURRY

3 tablespoons vegetable oil
1 large onion, sliced
3 cloves garlic, crushed
2 teaspoons grated fresh ginger
¾ teaspoon cayenne
½ teaspoon ground turmeric
2 teaspoons ground cumin
2 teaspoons ground coriander
1 teaspoon garam masala
4 cardamom pods, crushed
4 curry leaves, torn
3lb hokkaido, chopped
1 cup coconut milk

Heat oil in medium pan; cook onion, garlic and ginger, stirring, until onion is soft. Add spices, pods and leaves; cook, stirring, about 2 minutes or until fragrant.

Add pumpkin and coconut milk; bring to boil, simmer, covered, 10 minutes. Uncover; simmer 10 minutes or until sauce thickens and pumpkin is tender.

Serves 4 to 6.

■ Can be made a day ahead.
■ Storage: Covered, in refrigerator.
■ Freeze: Not suitable.
■ Microwave: Suitable.

Hokkaido. Large, glossy, dark-green with pale yellow speckles and deep yellow flesh; has a pleasant sweet flavor.

OPPOSITE: Pumpkin Curry.
ABOVE: Roasted Squash Puree.

GRATED SQUASH SALAD

1¹/₂lb Blue Hubbard squash,
  coarsely grated
¹/₄ cup chopped fresh cilantro
1¹/₂ tablespoons black mustard
  seeds

SOY LIME DRESSING
¹/₃ cup vegetable oil
1¹/₂ tablespoons soy sauce
1 tablespoon lime juice
1¹/₂ tablespoons brown sugar
¹/₂ teaspoon ground cumin

Combine squash, cilantro, seeds and three-quarters of the Soy Lime Dressing. Cover; refrigerate at least 30 minutes. Just before serving, drizzle remaining dressing over salad.
Soy Lime Dressing: Combine all ingredients in jar; shake well.

Serves 4.

▨ Best made on day of serving.
▨ Storage: Covered, in refrigerator.
▨ Freeze: Not suitable.

PUMPKIN PRIMAVERA SALAD

8oz asparagus
2 sugar pumpkins, sliced
8oz cherry tomatoes, halved
8oz pear tomatoes, halved
¹/₄ cup parmesan cheese, shaved

ITALIAN DRESSING
¹/₂ cup olive oil
3 tablespoons coarsely chopped
  fresh basil
1¹/₂ tablespoons white wine vinegar
1 clove garlic, coarsely chopped

Snap off and discard woody ends from asparagus; cut asparagus into 2¹/₂-inch lengths. Boil, steam or microwave asparagus until just tender; rinse under cold water. Pat dry with paper towels.

Boil, steam or microwave pumpkin until just tender; rinse under cold water. Pat dry with paper towels. Grill or barbecue pumpkin, in batches, until browned and tender.

Just before serving, gently mix pumpkin, tomatoes and asparagus with Italian Dressing in large bowl; scatter shaved parmesan over salad.
Italian Dressing: Blend or process all ingredients until smooth.

Serves 4.

▨ Italian Dressing can be made
  a day ahead.
▨ Storage: Covered, in refrigerator.
▨ Freeze: Not suitable.

LEFT FROM TOP: Grated Squash Salad; Pumpkin Primavera Salad.

Blue Hubbard squash: this large, pale grey-blue, ridged variety is usually sold in pre-cut wedges; good all-round performer.

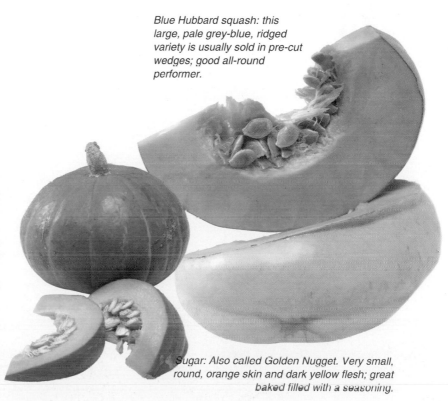

Sugar: Also called Golden Nugget. Very small, round, orange skin and dark yellow flesh; great baked filled with a seasoning.

Radicchio

A member of the chicory family, radicchio – along with arugula – is a common Italian salad green (the fact that it's a deep ruby-red in color notwithstanding). Its ingenious versatility comes into play when you discover that dramatic-looking radicchio, unlike other salad leaves, is just as good grilled or fried as it is eaten raw.

CHAR-GRILLED RADICCHIO PARCELS

Radicchio made its first appearance on most of our tables about the same time as did prosciutto, sun-dried tomatoes and bocconcini: this recipe combines the four in one sensational package.

1/4 cup olive oil
3oz sliced prosciutto, chopped
1 medium onion, chopped
2 cloves garlic, crushed
1/4 cup drained sun-dried tomatoes in oil, chopped
8oz bocconcini cheese, chopped
2 teaspoons drained capers, chopped
3 tablespoons chopped fresh basil
6 large radicchio leaves
3 tablespoons olive oil

Heat 1 1/2 tablespoons of the oil in medium pan; cook prosciutto, onion and garlic, stirring, until onion is soft and browned lightly, cool. Combine prosciutto mixture with tomatoes, bocconcini, capers and basil in medium bowl.

Boil, steam or microwave radicchio leaves briefly, until they are just limp; rinse leaves under cold water, pat dry with paper towels.

Place leaves on work surface. Divide filling mixture among leaves; roll up, folding in edges to enclose filling. Brush parcels all over with some of the remaining oil; cook in heated griddle pan or barbecue until browned and heated through, turning once during cooking. Serve drizzled with any remaining oil.

Serves 6.

■ Filling can be made a day ahead.
■ Storage: Covered, in refrigerator.
■ Freeze: Not suitable.
■ Microwave: Radicchio suitable.

Fork from Home & Garden on the Mall

Radicchio

LEFT: Char-Grilled Radicchio Parcels.
OPPOSITE: Pancetta Radicchio Salad with Anchovy Mayonnaise.

PANCETTA RADICCHIO SALAD WITH ANCHOVY MAYONNAISE

Use a tightly furled, medium-size head of radicchio with a weight in the vicinity of 8oz for this recipe.

3¹/₂ oz sliced pancetta
4 eggs
1 medium radicchio
1 large Belgian endive
¹/₂ cup parmesan cheese, shaved

GARLIC BASIL CROUTONS
¹/₂ small (about 6-inch long)
   baguette
4 tablespoons butter, melted
1 clove garlic, crushed
1¹/₂ tablespoons finely chopped
   fresh basil

ANCHOVY MAYONNAISE
1 egg
1¹/₂ tablespoons white wine vinegar
1 teaspoon stone ground mustard
8 drained anchovy fillets
³/₄ cup olive oil
¹/₄ cup buttermilk

Saute pancetta until crisp and browned; when cool, break into large pieces. Cover eggs with cold water in medium pan; bring to boil then simmer, uncovered, 5 minutes. Drain, shell and halve eggs.

Separate radicchio and endive leaves; place leaves in bowl. Drizzle with three-quarters of the Anchovy Mayonnaise, then top with pancetta, egg halves, parmesan, Garlic Basil Croutons and, last, the remaining mayonnaise.

Garlic Basil Croutons: Cut baguette into ¹/₄-inch slices; brush both sides of slices with combined butter, garlic and basil. Place in single layer on baking sheet; bake in 375°F oven for about 8 minutes or until browned and crisp.

Anchovy Mayonnaise: Blend or process egg, vinegar, mustard and anchovies until pureed. With motor operating, gradually pour in oil in thin stream; process until thick. Pour in buttermilk; process until combined.

Serves 6 to 8.

■ Garlic Basil Croutons and
   Anchovy Mayonnaise can be made a
   day ahead.
■ Storage: Croutons, in airtight
   container. Mayonnaise, covered,
   in refrigerator.
■ Freeze: Not suitable.
■ Microwave: Not suitable.

DAIKON AND PICKLED GINGER STIR-FRY

An everyday fixture at the Japanese table, we are now just starting to experience the wonderful flavor of this long, white radish.

1 large daikon
2oz pickled ginger, drained
1¹/₂ tablespoons peanut oil
2 green onions, finely sliced
**1¹/₂ tablespoons mirin
  [see Glossary]**
2 tablespoons rice vinegar
1 teaspoon wasabi paste
2 teaspoons soy sauce

Peel, top and tail daikon, cut into paper-thin 2¹/₂-inch-long strips. Rinse ginger under cold water; drain, chop roughly. Heat oil in wok or large pan; stir-fry daikon about 5 minutes or until just tender. Add ginger and onions; stir-fry 1 minute. Transfer daikon mixture to serving bowl; drizzle with combined remaining ingredients.

Serves 4 to 6.

■ Best made just before serving.
■ Freeze: Not suitable.
■ Microwave: Not suitable.

MOROCCAN RADISH AND ORANGE SALAD

The best way to get the symmetrically paper-thin slices of radish required for this recipe is by using a V-slicer [see Glossary] or mandoline.

1lb radishes, finely sliced
3 large oranges, segmented
¹/₃ cup shelled pistachios, toasted
¹/₄ cup chopped fresh chives
**2 teaspoons sumac [see Glossary]
  or tamarind concentrate**
¹/₄ cup orange juice
3 tablespoons olive oil
1¹/₂ tablespoons lemon juice
1 teaspoon sugar
¹/₂ teaspoon ground cumin
1 teaspoon white wine vinegar
1 clove garlic, crushed

Daikon Radish

Radish

Combine radish slices, oranges, nuts chives and sumac or the tamarind concentrate in large bowl; pour combined remaining ingredients over salad mixture. Toss salad gently; cover, refrigerate a least 1 hour before serving.

Serves 6.

■ Can be made 3 hours ahead.
■ Storage: Covered, in refrigerator.
■ Freeze: Not suitable.

*ABOVE: Daikon and Pickled Ginger Stir-Fr
OPPOSITE: Moroccan Radish
and Orange Salad.*

White Radish

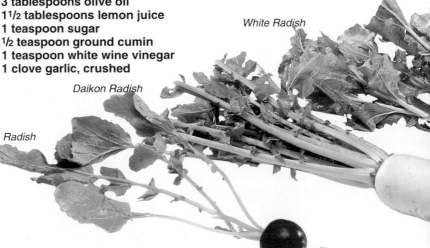

Radish

*When you were a child, what was summer without a
peppery radish and buttered white bread sandwich?
Round or elongated, red or white – but always piquant,
crunchy and clean-tasting – radishes warrant a closer
look than being just one of a crowded platter of crudités.*

RUTABAGA AND SWEET POTATO AU GRATIN

1lb rutabaga, sliced
8oz orange sweet potato, sliced
1 medium onion, sliced
3/4 cup grated cheddar cheese
1/4 cup grated parmesan cheese
3 tablespoons chopped fresh dill
2 teaspoons cracked black pepper
1/2 cup cream

Oil 10-cup shallow ovenproof dish. Layer half of the rutabaga, sweet potato and onion in prepared dish; sprinkle with half of the combined cheeses, dill and pepper. Repeat with remaining rutabaga, sweet potato and onion. Pour cream over top of vegetables; top with remaining cheese mixture. Bake, covered, in 350ºF oven 1 hour; uncover, bake about 30 minutes or until top is browned and vegetables are tender.

Serves 6.

■ Can be made a day ahead.
■ Storage: Covered, in refrigerator.
■ Freeze: Not suitable.
■ Microwave: Not suitable.

SPICED MASHED RUTABAGA

1/4 cup currants or raisins
1/4 cup orange juice
2lb rutabaga, chopped
2 teaspoons peanut oil
1 medium onion, chopped
2 cloves garlic, crushed
2 teaspoons ground cumin
2 teaspoons ground coriander
3 tablespoons chopped
 fresh cilantro

Combine currants and juice in small bowl; let stand 30 minutes. Drain; discard juice. Boil, steam or microwave rutabaga until tender; drain. Mash with potato masher in large bowl; keep rutabaga warm.

Heat oil in small pan; cook onion, garlic and ground spices, stirring, until onion is soft. Combine onion mixture, currants and cilantro with mashed rutabaga.

Serves 4.

■ Best made just before serving.
■ Freeze: Not suitable.
■ Microwave: Suitable.

ABOVE LEFT: Rutabaga and Sweet Potato Au Gratin.
LEFT: Spiced Mashed Rutabaga.
OPPOSITE: Hazelnut-Coated Rutabaga and Beet Croquettes.

Setting from House In Newtown

Rutabaga

Also known as swedes, the name rutabaga is a bastardization of an archaic Swedish word, rotabaggee. Sometimes confused with the turnip, the rutabaga is in fact a member of the cabbage family, and is eaten throughout winter in northern Europe, especially Scotland where, mashed with potatoes, it becomes tatties and neeps, traditionally accompanying haggis.

COOKING METHODS *Cooking times are based on 4 medium rutabagas, peeled, chopped into 1-inch pieces.*

• **BOIL** *Add rutabagas to large pan of boiling water; boil, uncovered, about 15 minutes or until tender. Drain.*

• **STEAM** *Place rutabagas in steamer basket; cook, uncovered, over pan of boiling water about 20 minutes or until tender. Drain.*

• **MICROWAVE** *Place rutabagas in large microwave-safe dish. Cover, microwave on HIGH (100%) about 8 minutes or until tender, pausing halfway during cooking time to stir. Drain.*

Tested in an 830-watt oven

HAZELNUT-COATED RUTABAGA AND BEET CROQUETTES

2lb rutabaga, roughly chopped
1 medium beet
1¹/₂ tablespoons olive oil
2 cloves garlic, crushed
1 medium onion, finely chopped
¹/₂ cup all-purpose flour
3 eggs, lightly beaten
¹/₂ cup milk
1¹/₄ cups fresh breadcrumbs
³/₄ cup hazelnuts, finely chopped
vegetable oil, for deep-frying

Boil, steam or microwave rutabaga and beet, separately, until tender; drain. Combine rutabaga and beet; mash in large bowl. Cool.

Heat oil in small pan; cook garlic and onion, stirring, until onion is soft. Stir garlic and onion into vegetable puree. When mixture is cool, shape 2 tablespoons of mixture into croquette; place on foil-lined tray. Repeat with remaining mixture; refrigerate about 30 minutes or until croquettes are firm.

Roll croquettes in flour, shake away excess; dip in combined eggs and milk, then combined breadcrumbs and nuts. Just before serving, deep fry croquettes in hot oil until golden brown; drain on paper towels.

Makes 18.

■ Uncooked croquettes can be made a day ahead.
■ Store: Covered, in refrigerator.
■ Freeze: Suitable.

Rutabaga

Spinach

Spinach is a world away, in looks and taste, from the leafy, green Swiss chard, with which it is often confused. While sometimes called English spinach, it was first cultivated in the Middle-East, taken to Spain and thence to America where it was popularized by Popeye! What a lineage! What an aristocrat of vegetables!

COOKING METHODS *Cooking times are based on 1 bunch (1lb) spinach, roots and about 2¹/₂-inches of lower stems cut off and discarded, leaves washed thoroughly.*

• **BOIL** *Add spinach to large pan of boiling water; remove immediately, refresh under cold water. Drain well.*

• **STEAM** *Place spinach in steamer basket; cook, covered, over pan of simmering water about 3 minutes or until just wilted, tossing halfway through cooking time. Drain.*

• **MICROWAVE** *Place spinach in large microwave-safe bowl. Cover, microwave on HIGH (100%) about 3 minutes or until just wilted; refresh under cold water. Drain well.*

Tested in an 850-watt oven

GARLICKY ONIONY SPINACH

Dried onion flakes are available from most supermarkets.

1¹/₂ tablespoons vegetable oil
5 cloves garlic, thinly sliced
2 bunches spinach (trimmed as described at left)
2 teaspoons cornstarch
¹/₂ cup chicken stock
2 teaspoons soy sauce
3 tablespoons onion flakes, toasted

Heat oil in wok or large pan; cook garlic, stirring, until it starts to brown. Add spinach and blended cornstarch, stock and sauce; cook, stirring, until spinach is just wilted and sauce boils and thickens slightly. Sprinkle with toasted onion flakes.

Serves 4 to 6.

■ Best made just before serving.
■ Freeze: Not suitable.
■ Microwave: Not suitable.

Spinach

Spinach

CREAMED SPINACH

We used creme fraiche here, but light sour cream can be substituted.

1¹/₂ tablespoons butter
2 bunches spinach (trimmed as
    described on previous page)
1¹/₂ tablespoons olive oil
1 large onion, chopped
5 slices prosciutto, chopped
2 cloves garlic, crushed
³/₄ cup creme fraiche
¹/₄ cup chopped fresh chives
¹/₄ teaspoon ground nutmeg

Heat butter in large pan; cook spinach, covered, stirring occasionally, until just wilted. Drain; gently squeeze spinach to remove excess liquid.

Heat oil in same pan; cook onion, prosciutto and garlic, stirring, until the prosciutto is browned and crisp. Add spinach and remaining ingredients; cook, stirring, until heated through.

Serves 6.

- Best made just before serving.
- Freeze: Not suitable.
- Microwave: Not suitable.

SPINACH SALAD WITH TOFFEE PECANS AND BLUE CHEESE

¼ cup sugar
½ cup pecans
6oz baby spinach leaves
½ cup olive oil
3 tablespoons white wine vinegar
½ teaspoon sugar
2oz creamy blue-vein cheese
1 clove garlic, crushed

Heat sugar in shallow pan, without stirring, until golden brown; mix nuts with sugar in pan until well coated. Transfer nut mixture to oiled baking sheet; cool then chop roughly.

Just before serving, gently toss toffee pecans and spinach with combined remaining ingredients.

Serves 4 to 6.

■ Toffee Pecans can be made a day ahead.
■ Storage: In airtight container.
■ Freeze: Not suitable.
■ Microwave: Not suitable.

SPINACH CAESAR SALAD

6 bacon slices, chopped
½ loaf unsliced white bread
1½ tablespoons olive oil
12oz baby spinach leaves
4 eggs, hard-boiled, quartered
3 tablespoons chopped fresh chives
⅓ cup parmesan cheese, shaved

SPINACH DRESSING
4oz baby spinach leaves
1 egg yolk
1½ tablespoons white wine vinegar
1 clove garlic, crushed
3 anchovy fillets
2 teaspoons Dijon mustard
½ teaspoon sugar
3 teaspoons lemon juice
⅓ cup vegetable oil
¼ cup buttermilk

Cook bacon in heated dry pan, stirring, until crisp; drain on paper towels.

Remove breadcrust; cut bread lengthwise into 1-inch slices, then into cubes; toss cubes and oil in medium bowl, place on baking sheet. Bake in 350ºF oven about 10 minutes or until browned lightly, turning once.

Gently toss spinach, bacon, bread cubes, eggs, chives and half the cheese in a large bowl. Arrange salad on serving platter; drizzle with Spinach Dressing, sprinkle with remaining cheese.

Spinach Dressing: Boil, steam or microwave spinach until just wilted; cool. Squeeze out excess moisture; roughly chop spinach. Blend or process egg yolk, vinegar, garlic, anchovies, mustard, sugar and juice until pureed. With motor operating, gradually pour in oil; process until thick. Add buttermilk and spinach; process until smooth.

Serves 6.

■ Best made just before serving.
■ Freeze: Not suitable.

OPPOSITE ABOVE: Creamed Spinach.
OPPOSITE BELOW: Spinach Salad with Toffee Pecans and Blue Cheese.
BELOW: Spinach Caesar Salad.

Sweet potatoes

Few vegetables are so often confused as sweet potatoes and yams. Although they come fro different families and continents (sweet potatoes are native to the Americas, yams to Africa), what these tubers share is what counts: gorgeous shades of orange flesh, rich nutrient content, and a sweet flavor that lends itself to every course from soup to desser

Sweet Potato

COOKING METHODS *Cooking times are based on 2 large sweet potatoes, peeled, sliced into 3/4 inch rounds.*

• BOIL Add sweet potatoes to large pan of boiling water; cook, uncovered, about 15 minutes or until tender. Drain.

• STEAM Place sweet potatoes in steamer basket; cook, covered, over pan of simmering water about 16 minutes or until tender. Drain.

• MICROWAVE Place sweet potatoes and 2 tablespoons water in large microwave-safe dish. Cover, microwave on HIGH (100%) about 10 minutes or until tender, pausing halfway during cooking time to stir. Drain.

Tested in an 850-watt oven

SWEET POTATO AND BROCCOLI STIR-FRY

3 medium orange sweet potatoes, sliced
2 cups broccoli florets
1¹/₂ tablespoons peanut oil
2 large onions, sliced
2 cloves garlic, crushed
2 teaspoons sambal oelek

CUMIN YOGURT DRESSING
¹/₂ cup yogurt
¹/₂ teaspoon ground coriander
1 teaspoon ground cumin
1¹/₂ tablespoons water
3 tablespoons lemon juice

Boil, steam or microwave sweet potatoes and broccoli florets, separately, until almost tender; drain.

Meanwhile, heat oil in wok or large pan; stir-fry onions, garlic and sambal oelek until onions are browned lightly.

Add sweet potatoes and broccoli; stir-fry until vegetables are heated through. Just before serving, drizzle with Cumin Yogurt Dressing.

Cumin Yogurt Dressing: Combine all ingredients in small bowl.

Serves 6 to 8.

■ Cumin Yogurt Dressing can be made a day ahead.
■ Storage: Covered, in refrigerator.
■ Freeze: Not suitable.

ABOVE: Sweet Potatoes and Broccoli Stir-Fry.
OPPOSITE FROM TOP: Honey Mustard-Glazed Sweet Potatoes; Cheese and Veggie Burgers.

HONEY MUSTARD-GLAZED SWEET POTATO

2 large orange sweet potatoes
2 medium onions, halved
1/2 cup honey
3 tablespoons balsamic vinegar
3 tablespoons stone ground
   mustard
11/2 tablespoons water
11/2 tablespoons peanut oil
11/2 tablespoons grated fresh ginger

Slice sweet potatoes into 1/2-inch rounds. Place sweet potatoes and onions in large bowl; toss with combined honey, vinegar, mustard, water, oil and ginger. Drain vegetables; reserve honey-mustard mixture.

Place vegetables on wire rack over oil-covered oven tray; bake in 400ºF oven 20 minutes, brushing frequently with honey-mustard mixture. Turn vegetables; bake, about 15 minutes or until vegetables are browned lightly, continuing to brush with honey-mustard mixture during cooking.

Serves 4 to 6.

■ Best made just before serving.
■ Freeze: Not suitable.
■ Microwave: Not suitable.

CHEESE AND VEGGIE BURGERS

1 medium orange sweet potato,
   chopped
1 large potato, chopped
1 large onion, chopped
1/4 cup vegetable oil
1/3 cup grated cheddar cheese
3oz green beans, chopped
1/4 cup fresh breadcrumbs
1/2 cup cornmeal

Combine sweet potato, potato, onion and 11/2 tablespoons of the oil in shallow baking dish; bake, covered, in 350ºF oven 30 minutes. Uncover, bake for a further 20 minutes or until vegetables are just tender. Transfer mixture to large bowl; mash until smooth. Stir in cheese, beans and breadcrumbs.

Sprinkle baking sheet with half the cornmeal. Divide vegetable mixture into 8 portions; press oiled metal 3-inch egg ring into 1 portion, lift onto oven tray using spatula. Sprinkle cornmeal over burger; carefully remove egg ring. Repeat with remaining portions of vegetable mixture.

Heat remaining oil in large pan; cook burgers, in batches, until browned both sides. Drain on paper towels.

Makes 8.

■ Burgers best made just before
   serving. Vegetable mix can be made
   a day ahead.
■ Storage: Covered, in refrigerator.
■ Freeze: Not suitable.
■ Microwave: Not suitable.

Bowl from Villeroy & Boch

Plates from Villeroy & Boch

Swiss chard

Swiss chard can be labeled spinach, seakale, blettes or silverbeet, depending on which part of the world you find it in. A hard-working vegetable, both Swiss chard's sturdy dark-green leaf and thick white stem, used together or separately, can be presented in a plethora of different ways, not least of which is dressed simply in your favorite vinaigrette.

COOKING METHODS *Cooking times are based on 1lb Swiss chard, white stems cut off and discarded, leaves washed thoroughly.*

• **BOIL** *Add whole leaves to large pan of boiling water; boil, uncovered, about 2 minutes or until tender. Drain.*

• **STEAM** *Place chopped leaves in steamer basket; cook, covered, over pan of simmering water about 4 minutes or until tender. Drain.*

• **MICROWAVE** *Place whole leaves in large microwave-safe dish. Cover, microwave on HIGH (100%) about 4 minutes or until tender, pausing halfway during cooking time to stir. Drain.*
Tested in an 850-watt oven

Swiss chard

LEFT FROM TOP: *Swiss chard Dal; Swiss Chard and Potato Puree.*
OPPOSITE: *Baby Swiss Chard with Raspberry Vinaigrette.*

SWISS CHARD DAL

1 cup red lentils
1 large onion
3 tablespoons ghee or
**   clarified butter**
3 cloves garlic, crushed
1¹/₂ tablespoons grated fresh ginger
1¹/₂ tablespoons Madras curry paste
14oz can tomatoes,
**   undrained, crushed**
¹/₂ cup vegetable stock
1lb Swiss chard, stems discarded,
**   leaves chopped**
1¹/₂ tablespoons lemon juice

Wash lentils under cold water; drain. Cut onion in half lengthwise then into wedges. Heat ghee in large pan; cook onion, garlic and ginger, stirring, about 5 minutes or until onion is soft. Add curry paste; cook, stirring, about 2 minutes or until fragrant. Stir in lentils, tomatoes and stock; simmer, covered, over low heat for about 30 minutes or until lentils are tender, stirring occasionally. Add the Swiss chard; cook, stirring, until chard is just wilted. Stir in lemon juice.

Serves 4 to 6.

■ Best made just before serving.
■ Freeze: Not suitable.
■ Microwave: Not suitable.

SWISS CHARD AND POTATO PUREE

Buy the best mashing potato you can find for this recipe – try using yukon gold or creamers [see Potatoes] if they're available.

2lb potatoes, chopped
4 tablespoons butter
1 small onion, chopped
8 anchovy fillets
¹/₂ cup milk
2lb Swiss chard, stems discarded,
**   leaves finely shredded**
3 tablespoons cream

Boil, steam or microwave potatoes until tender; drain. Push potatoes through coarse sieve into large bowl; cover to keep warm. Heat butter in medium pan; cook onion and anchovies, stirring, until onion is soft and anchovies break up. Stir onion mixture and warmed milk into potatoes in serving bowl; cover.

Boil, steam or microwave chard until just wilted; drain. Squeeze out excess liquid from chard; combine with cream in medium bowl. Gently swirl chard mixture through potato mixture.

Serves 4 to 6.

■ Best made just before serving.
■ Freeze: Not suitable.

BABY SWISS CHARD WITH RASPBERRY VINAIGRETTE

You can substitute frozen raspberries, thawed and well-drained, if fresh ones aren't available.

5oz baby Swiss chard leaves
2oz mesclun [see Lettuce]
¹/₂ cup fresh raspberries
¹/₃ cup chopped hazelnuts, toasted
1 small red onion, thinly sliced
RASPBERRY VINAIGRETTE
¹/₂ cup fresh raspberries
¹/₃ cup orange juice
1¹/₂ tablespoons hazelnut oil
1¹/₂ tablespoons vegetable oil
1 teaspoon sugar

Gently toss all salad ingredients with Raspberry Vinaigrette in medium bowl.
Raspberry Vinaigrette: Blend or process all ingredients until smooth; strain into jar.

Serves 4.

■ Salad must be made just before serving. Raspberry Vinaigrette can be made a day ahead.
■ Storage: Covered, in refrigerator.
■ Freeze: Not suitable.

Cherry

Plum

Vine-
Ripened

Pear

Tomatoes

You say tomaytoes while I say tomahtoes, but we nevertheless agree on the so-called love apple's qualities: amazing versatility, fabulous flavor and loaded with vitamins. Another food that originated in the New World, tomato seeds were taken to Europe by the Spaniards... and Mediterranean cooking never looked back.

TOMATO BRUSCHETTA SALAD

1/2 loaf Italian bread
1/4 cup olive oil
3 medium tomatoes,
   roughly chopped
1 large red onion, roughly chopped
4oz arugula, torn
1 cup parmesan cheese, shaved
1/3 cup shredded fresh basil
1/3 cup olive oil
3 tablespoons red wine vinegar
1 clove garlic, crushed
1 teaspoon sugar

Cut bread into 1 1/2-inch pieces. Heat oil in large pan; cook bread pieces, stirring, until browned and crisp, drain on paper towels.

Just before serving, gently toss warm bread, tomatoes, onion, arugula, parmesan and basil with combined remaining ingredients in large bowl.

Serves 6.

■ Best made just before serving.
■ Freeze: Not suitable.
■ Microwave: Not suitable.

PENNE WITH SAUTEED TOMATOES AND FETA

8oz penne pasta
1/4 cup olive oil
2 medium onions, sliced
2 cloves garlic, crushed
3 tablespoons pine nuts
8oz cherry tomatoes
8oz pear tomatoes
1 teaspoon cracked black pepper
12oz feta cheese, chopped
1 1/2 tablespoons chopped
   fresh oregano

Add pasta to large pan of boiling water. Boil, uncovered, until just tender; drain.

Heat oil in large pan; cook onions, garlic and nuts, stirring, until onions are soft and nuts browned. Add both tomatoes and pepper; cook, stirring, until tomatoes just begin to soften. Stir in pasta, feta and oregano until mixture is heated through and cheese softens.

Serves 6.

■ Best made just before serving.
■ Freeze: Not suitable.
■ Microwave: Not suitable.

ROASTED TOMATOES WITH BALSAMIC DRESSING

12 large plum tomatoes,
   halved lengthwise
1/2 cup olive oil
1 1/2 tablespoons sugar
2 cloves garlic, crushed
1 teaspoon salt
1 teaspoon cracked black pepper
1 1/2 tablespoons balsamic vinegar
1 1/2 tablespoons shredded
   fresh basil

Place tomatoes, cut side up, on wire rack in baking dish. Brush with half of the combined oil, sugar, garlic, salt and pepper. Bake, uncovered, in 350ºF oven about 1 1/2 hours or until tomatoes are softened and browned lightly.

Drizzle combined remaining oil and vinegar over tomatoes; scatter with basil.

Serves 6.

■ Can be made 3 days ahead.
■ Storage: Covered, in refrigerator.
■ Freeze: Not suitable.
■ Microwave: Not suitable.

OPPOSITE FROM TOP: Tomato Bruschetta Salad; Penne with Sauteed Tomatoes and Feta.
ABOVE: Roasted Tomatoes with Balsamic Dressing.

115

COOKING METHODS *Cooking times are based on 4 medium turnips, thickly peeled, roughly chopped. (Thickly peeling turnips removes the slightly bitter taste they sometimes have.)*

• **BOIL** *Add turnips to large pan of boiling water; boil, uncovered, about 9 minutes or until tender. Drain.*

• **STEAM** *Place turnips in steamer basket; cook, covered, over pan of simmering water about 12 minutes or until tender. Drain.*

• **MICROWAVE** *Place turnips and 1 tablespoon water in large microwave-safe dish. Cover, microwave on HIGH (100%) about 6 minutes or until tender, pausing halfway during cooking time to stir. Drain.*

Tested in an 850-watt oven

CREAMY TURNIP PUREE

If small baby turnips are available, use them in this recipe for their delicate, sweet flavor.

1¹⁄₄lb turnips, chopped
5 medium potatoes, chopped
³⁄₄ cup creme fraiche
¹⁄₃ cup grated parmesan cheese

CARAMELIZED ONIONS
4 tablespoons butter
2 medium onions, finely sliced
3 tablespoons sugar
1¹⁄₂ tablespoons malt vinegar

Boil, steam or microwave turnips and potatoes, separately, until tender; drain. Combine vegetables; mash with creme fraiche and parmesan in large bowl. Stir Caramelized Onions through puree.
Caramelized Onions: Heat butter in medium pan; cook onions, stirring, about 10 minutes or until soft. Add sugar and vinegar; stir over heat about 10 minutes or until onions are caramelized.

Serves 6.

■ Best made just before serving.
■ Freeze: Not suitable.
■ Microwave: Onions not suitable

Tiles from Country Floors

Turnip

116

Turnips

The homely turnip's sweet bitterness marries so well with traditional meat dishes that it can easily displace a potato. Plus, it's been re-invented to gain contemporary cachet by scenting a Moroccan stew, masquerading in a puree or nestling in a bunch of purple-tinged miniatures.

ROASTED TURNIPS

2lb turnips, roughly chopped
8 cloves garlic, unpeeled
1¹/₂ tablespoons brown sugar
3 tablespoons olive oil
1 teaspoon cumin seeds

Toss turnips and garlic with combined remaining ingredients in a large bowl. Place in baking dish; bake, uncovered, in 400ºF oven for about 30 minutes or until browned lightly, stirring occasionally.

Serves 4 to 6.

■ Best made just before serving.
■ Freeze: Not suitable.
■ Microwave: Not suitable.

TURNIP RATATOUILLE

2 medium eggplants
¹/₄ cup olive oil
2 cloves garlic, crushed
2lb turnips, roughly chopped
2 small red bell peppers, roughly
**   chopped**
2 medium green zucchini, chopped
2 large yellow zucchini, chopped
2 14oz cans tomatoes,
**   undrained, crushed**
3 tablespoons tomato paste
1¹/₂ tablespoons capers, rinsed,
**   drained, chopped**
3 tablespoons dry red wine
¹/₄ cup firmly packed basil,
**   shredded**

Cut eggplants into ¹/₂-inch slices; quarter slices. Heat oil in large heavy-based pan; cook eggplant and garlic, stirring, about 5 minutes or until just tender and browned lightly. Add turnips, bell pepper, zucchini, tomatoes, paste, capers and wine; simmer, covered, about 30 minutes or until vegetables are tender. Stir in half the basil; sprinkle

Dishes from Opus; tiles from Country Floors

remaining half over top of ratatouille just before serving.

Serves 8.

■ Can be made a day ahead.
■ Storage: Covered, in refrigerator.
■ Freeze: Not suitable.
■ Microwave: Not suitable.

OPPOSITE: Creamy Turnip Puree.
ABOVE FROM TOP: Roasted Turnips;
Turnip Ratatouille.

Zucchini and squash

Known collectively as summer squash (to distinguish them from winter squashes, like pumpkins which have inedible seeds and skins), zucchini, pattipan or pattypan, and marrows can be eaten in their entirety – even their flowers! Available year round, their adaptability and versatility have made them almost as popular here as they are in southern Europe.

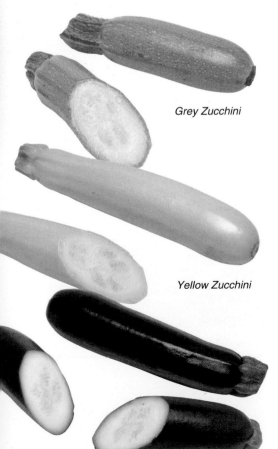

Grey Zucchini

Yellow Zucchini

Zucchini

COOKING METHODS *Cooking times are based on 4 medium zucchini, trimmed, halved crosswise.*

• **BOIL** *Add zucchini to medium pan of boiling water; boil, uncovered, about 4 minutes or until tender. Drain.*

• **STEAM** *Place zucchini in steamer basket; cook, covered, over pan of simmering water about 6 minutes or until tender. Drain.*

• **MICROWAVE** *Place zucchini and 2 tablespoons water in medium microwave-safe dish. Cover, microwave on HIGH (100%) about 5 minutes, pausing halfway during cooking time to stir. Drain.*
Tested in an 850-watt oven

Green Zucchini

DEEP-FRIED RICOTTA-FILLED ZUCCHINI FLOWERS

Try growing your own zucchini (or making friends with a farmer) so that you can pick flowers with a new zucchini just forming – the taste is unforgettable.

18 zucchini flowers
½ cup all-purpose flour
3 tablespoons cornstarch
3 tablespoons cornmeal
½ teaspoon sugar
2 egg whites
½ cup water
vegetable oil, for deep-frying

RICOTTA FILLING
1 cup ricotta cheese
2 green onions, finely chopped
3 tablespoons pine nuts, toasted
1½ tablespoons chopped
**   fresh basil**
2 cloves garlic, crushed

Remove and discard flower stamens from center of flowers; divide Ricotta Filling ingredients among the flowers.

Twist flower petals to enclose filling. Sift flour, cornstarch, cornmeal and sugar into medium bowl; stir in combined egg whites and water, mix to a smooth batter. Dip flowers in batter to coat completely. Heat oil in large pan; deep-fry flowers, in batches, until browned lightly and crisp. Drain on paper towels.
Ricotta Filling: Combine all ingredients in small bowl.

Serves 4 to 6.

■ Zucchini Flowers must be made just before serving. Ricotta Filling can be made 3 hours ahead.
■ Storage: Covered, in refrigerator.
■ Freeze: Not suitable.
■ Microwave: Not suitable.

BAKED ZUCCHINI AND TOMATOES

6 medium zucchini
4 medium plum tomatoes
1 medium onion
3 cloves garlic, crushed
¼ cup chopped fresh oregano
¼ cup olive oil
⅓ cup drained sun-dried tomatoes in oil, chopped

Halve each zucchini crosswise; quarter each half lengthwise. Quarter tomatoes lengthwise. Halve onion; cut halves into wedges. Gently toss zucchini, tomato, onion, garlic and oregano with oil in large bowl to coat. Place in baking dish; bake, covered, in 400ºF oven 20 minutes. Stir in sun-dried tomato pieces; bake, uncovered, 15 minutes or until zucchini are just tender.

Serves 6.

■ Best made just before serving.
■ Freeze: Not suitable.
■ Microwave: Not suitable.

TUNISIAN-STYLE SQUASH WITH COUSCOUS

Some green grocers call pattipan squash scallopini, and they usually come in both a pale green and yellow variety, just like zucchini.

3 medium green zucchini
3 medium yellow zucchini
6 medium green pattipan squash
6 medium yellow pattipan squash
1½ tablespoons ground cumin
2 cloves garlic, crushed
¼ cup hot chili sauce
3 tablespoons olive oil
1 cup couscous
1 cup boiling water
1½ tablespoons butter

Halve zucchini crosswise, then into slices lengthwise; slice squash thinly. Gently toss zucchini, squash, cumin, garlic, sauce with oil in large bowl to coat. Cook vegetables, in batches, in heated oiled griddle pan (or grill or barbecue) until browned and tender.

Meanwhile, combine remaining ingredients in heatproof bowl; cover, let stand 5 minutes or until water is absorbed. Fluff couscous with fork before serving with vegetables.

Serves 4 to 6.

■ Best made just before serving.
■ Freeze: Not suitable.
■ Microwave: Not suitable.

CLOCKWISE FROM LEFT: Tunisian-Style Squash with Couscous; Baked Zucchini and Tomatoes; Deep-Fried Ricotta-Filled Zucchini Flowers.

Squash

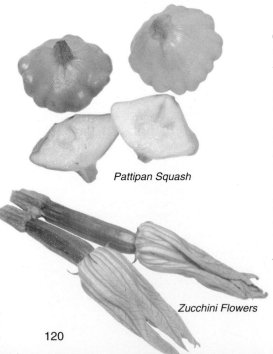

Pattipan Squash

Zucchini Flowers

COOKING METHODS *Cooking times are based on 1lb pattipan squash, trimmed, quartered.*

• **BOIL** *Add squash to medium pan of boiling water; boil, uncovered, about 4 minutes or until tender. Drain.*

• **STEAM** *Place squash in steamer basket; cook, covered, over pan of simmering water about 6 minutes or until tender. Drain.*

• **MICROWAVE** *Place squash and 2 tablespoons water in medium microwave-safe dish. Cover, microwave on HIGH (100%) about 4 minutes, pausing halfway during cooking time to stir. Drain.*

Tested in an 850-watt oven

ZUCCHINI AND RADISH SUMMER SALAD

6 medium zucchini
8oz radishes, thinly sliced
4 green onions, chopped
1 tablespoon chopped drained
   pickled ginger
3 tablespoons mirin [see Glossary]
1½ tablespoons rice vinegar
few drops sesame oil

Using a V-slicer [see Glossary], cut zucchini into thin strips. Gently toss zucchini, radishes, onions and ginger with combined remaining ingredients in large bowl; mix well.

Serves 4 to 6.

■ Best made just before serving.
■ Freeze: Not suitable.
■ Microwave: Not suitable.

ZUCCHINI AND CABBAGE STIR-FRY

3 tablespoons butter
2 cloves garlic, crushed
2 small fresh red chilies, chopped
6 medium zucchini, coarsely grated
8oz Chinese cabbage,
    finely chopped
1¹/₂ tablespoons lemon juice

Heat butter in wok or large pan; cook garlic and chilies, stirring, until garlic is fragrant. Add remaining ingredients; stir-fry until just cooked and hot.

Serves 6 to 8.

■ Best made just before serving.
■ Freeze: Not suitable.
■ Microwave: Not suitable.

Bowl from Dinosaur Designs

ZUCCHINI TIMBALES WITH LIME-BUTTERMILK CREAM

4 medium zucchini, coarsely grated
1 medium apple, unpeeled,
    coarsely grated
1¹/₂ tablespoons chopped
    fresh mint
2 teaspoons lime juice

LIME-BUTTERMILK CREAM
1 cup buttermilk
¹/₄ cup mayonnaise
2 teaspoons grated lime rind
3 tablespoons lime juice
1 teaspoon cream style horseradish
1 teaspoon sugar

Oil 4 ¹/₂-cup molds, line bases with baking paper. Combine all timbale ingredients in medium bowl; drain mixture in sieve, pressing out as much liquid as possible. Press mixture firmly into prepared molds; turn onto individual serving plates. Serve with Lime-Buttermilk Cream.
Lime-Buttermilk Cream: Combine all ingredients in small bowl; whisk well.

Serves 4.

■ Timbales best made just before serving. Lime-Buttermilk Cream can be made a day ahead.
■ Storage: Covered, in refrigerator.
■ Freeze: Not suitable.
■ Microwave: Not suitable.

Plate from Dinosaur Designs

OPPOSITE: Zucchini and Radish Summer Salad.
ABOVE: Zucchini and Cabbage Stir-Fry.
LEFT: Zucchini Timbales with Lime-Buttermilk Cream.

Garam masala

Walnuts

Saffron

Hazelnut

Thyme

Rosemary

Marjoram

Dill

Curly Parsley

Cilantro

Italian parsley

Mint

Oregano

Basil

Curry leaves

Lemon grass

Glossary

Here are some terms, names and alternatives to help everyone use and understand our recipes perfectly.

ALLSPICE: also known as Jamaican pepper or pimento; available whole or ground. Tastes like a blend of cinnamon, clove and nutmeg.

BAKING PAPER: also known as parchment, silicon paper or non-stick baking paper; not to be confused with greaseproof or wax(ed) paper. Used to line pans; can also be used to make piping bags.

BEAN SPROUTS: also known as bean shoots; tender new growths of assorted beans and seeds germinated for consumption as sprouts. The most readily available are mung bean, soy bean, alfalfa and snow pea sprouts.

BLACK ONION SEEDS: see SEEDS.

BREADCRUMBS:
Fresh: one- or two-day-old bread made into crumbs by grating, blending or processing.
Packaged: fine-textured, crunchy, purchased, white breadcrumbs.

BUTTER: use salted or unsalted ("sweet") butter; 8 tablespoons is equal to 1 stick butter.

BUTTERMILK: low-fat milk cultured with bacteria to give it a slightly sour, tangy taste; low-fat yogurt can be substituted.

CAJUN SEASONING: used to impart a traditional spicy Cajun flavor to fried foods; this packaged blend of assorted herbs and spices can include paprika, basil, onion, cayenne, fennel, thyme or tarragon.

CANNELLINI BEANS: small, dried white bean similar in appearance and flavor to other *phaseolus vulgaris*: great northern, navy and haricot beans.

CAPERS: the grey-green buds of a warm-climate (usually Mediterranean) shrub sold either dried and salted, or pickled in a vinegar brine; used to enhance sauces and dressings with their piquancy.

CARDAMOM: native to India and used extensively in its cuisine; can be purchased in pod, seed or ground form. Has a distinctive aromatic, sweetly rich flavor and is one of the world's most expensive spices.

CHEESE:
Blue vein: mold-treated cheese mottled with blue veining; many varieties, ranging from firm, crumbly and strong-flavored to mild, creamy and brie-like.
Bocconcini: small rounds of fresh "baby" mozzarella, a delicate, semi-soft, white cheese traditionally made in Italy from buffalo's milk. Spoils rapidly so must be kept under refrigeration, in brine, for 1 or 2 days at most.
Brie: buttery soft cheese with an edible, chalk-like, white-mold rind; originally from France but now manufactured locally. Very high fat content; when ripe and ready to eat, the center of this cheese should be quite runny.

Cheddar: the most common cow's milk "tasty" cheese; should be aged, hard and have a pronounced bite flavor.
Feta: Greek in origin; a crumbly goat's or sheep's milk cheese with a sharp, salty taste.
Gruyere: a Swiss cheese having small holes and a nutty, slightly salty flavor.
Parmesan: a sharp-tasting, dry, hard cheese, made from skim or part skim milk and aged for at least a year before being sold. The best quality is Parmigiano Reggiano, from Italy, aged a minimum of three years.
Ricotta: a sweet, fairly moist, fresh curd cheese having a low-fat content.

CHILIES: available in many different types and sizes. Use rubber gloves when seeding and chopping to avoid burning your skin. Discard seeds to lessen the heat level.
Powder: the Asian variety is the hottest, made from ground chilies; it can be used as a substitute for fresh chilies in the proportion of 1/2 teaspoon ground chili powder to 1 medium chopped fresh chili.
Sauce: our recipes used a hot Chinese variety made of chilies, salt and vinegar. Use sparingly, increasing amounts to taste.
Sweet chili sauce: a comparatively mild, Thai-type, commercial sauce made from red chilies, sugar, garlic and vinegar.

CHINESE BROCCOLI: also known as gai lum.
CHINESE CABBAGE: also known as Peking cabbage or wong bok.
CHINESE WATER SPINACH: also known as swamp spinach, ung choy, kang kong.
CHOY SUM: also known as flowering bok choy or flowering white cabbage.
CILANTRO: also known as coriander or Chinese parsley; bright-green, leafy herb with a pungent flavor. Often stirred into a dish just before serving for maximum impact.
COCONUT MILK: pure, unsweetened; available in cans.
COUSCOUS: a fine, grain-like cereal product, originally from North Africa; made of semolina.
CREAM: fresh pouring cream (minimum fat content 35%).
Sour: a thick, commercially cultured soured cream (minimum fat content 35%).
CREME FRAICHE: a fresh matured cream that has been commercially lightly soured (minimum fat content 35%); available in cartons from delicatessens and supermarkets. To make creme fraiche, combine 1 cup cream with 1 cup sour cream in bowl; cover, stand at room temperature until mixture thickens. This will take 1 or 2 days, depending on room temperature; refrigerate once fermented. Makes 2 cups.

Pistachios

Pine nuts

Pecans

Slivered almonds

Sliced almonds

Macadamias

CURRY LEAVES: shiny, bright-green, sharp-ended leaves used, fresh or dried, in cooking, especially in Indian curries.

CURRY PASTE: some recipes in this book call for commercially prepared pastes of various strengths and flavors, ranging from the mild Tikka and medium Madras to the fiery Vindaloo. Use whichever one you feel suits your spice-level tolerance.

DAL: an Indian term that describes both legumes, dried peas and beans, and the range of spicy, stew-like dishes containing them.

EGGS: some recipes in this book call for raw or barely cooked eggs; exercise caution if there is a salmonella problem in your area.

ENGLISH SPINACH: correct name for spinach.

FENNEL: also known as finocchio or anise.

FETTUCCINE: A ribbon pasta, about 1/4-inch in width, made from durum wheat semolina and egg, available fresh or dried, plain or flavored with herbs, pepper or vegetable essences.

FISH SAUCE: also called nam pla or nuoc nam; made from pulverized, salted, fermented fish, most often anchovies. Has a pungent smell and strong taste; use sparingly. There are many different fish sauces on the market, and the intensity of flavor varies.

FIVE-SPICE POWDER: a fragrant mixture of ground cinnamon, cloves, star anise, Sichuan pepper and fennel seeds.

GARAM MASALA: a blend of spices, originally from Northern India, based on cardamom, cinnamon, cloves, coriander and cumin. Sometimes chili is added.

GARBANZOS: also called chickpeas, hummus or channa; an irregularly round, sandy-colored legume used extensively in Mediterranean and Latin cooking.

GARLIC: a bulb contains many cloves which can be crushed, sliced, chopped, or used whole, peeled or unpeeled.

GELATINE: (also called gelatin) the recipes in this book use powdered gelatine. It is also available in sheet form, called leaf gelatine.

GHEE: clarified butter; with the milk solids removed, this semi-solid fat can be heated to a high temperature without burning.

GHERKIN: also known as cornichon; both the name of a kind of tiny, young, dark-green cucumber and the term to describe it after it has been pickled with herbs in vinegar.

GINGER:

Fresh: also known as green or root ginger; the thick gnarled root of a tropical plant. Can be kept, peeled, in dry sherry in a jar and refrigerated, or frozen in an airtight container.

Pickled pink: available, packaged, from Asian groceries; pickled, paper-thin shavings of ginger in a mixture of vinegar, sugar and natural coloring.

HERBS: when specified, we used 1 teaspoon dried (not ground) herbs as being the equivalent of 3 teaspoons (1 tablespoon) chopped fresh herbs.

HOISIN SAUCE: a thick, sweet and spicy Chinese paste made from salted, fermented soy beans, onions and garlic; used as a marinade or baste, or to accent stir-fries and barbecued or roasted foods.

HORSERADISH, CREAM STYLE: a creamy paste of grated horseradish, vinegar, oil and sugar, often used as a condiment.

KALONJI: see SEEDS

KITCHEN STRING: be certain to use string made from a natural material specifically for use in cooking; a synthetic string will melt if used over heat or in the oven.

LEMON GRASS: a tall, clumping, lemon-smelling and tasting, sharp-edged grass; the white lower part of each stem is chopped and used in Asian cooking or for making tea.

MAPLE SYRUP: distilled sap of the maple tree. Maple-flavored syrup or pancake syrup is made from cane sugar and artificial maple flavoring; is a poor substitute for the real thing.

MIRIN: a sweet, low-alcohol rice wine used in Japanese cooking; sometimes referred to simply as rice wine. Do not confuse with sake, the Japanese rice wine made for drinking.

MORTADELLA: a delicately spiced and smoked Italian sausage made of pork, beef and pork fat.

MUSTARD, STONE GROUND: a coarse-grain mustard made of crushed mustard seeds and Dijon-style French mustard.

NOODLES, FRIED: Crispy egg noodles, packaged (commonly a 3oz can).

NUTS:

Almonds: Blanched, skins removed; Sliced, paper-thin slices; Ground, also called almond meal; Slivered, small lengthwise-cut pieces.

Hazelnuts: also known as filberts; plump, grape-size, rich, sweet nut having a brown inedible skin that is removed by rubbing heated nuts together vigorously in a teatowel.

Macadamias: native to Australia and now grown extensively in Hawaii. A rich, buttery nut that should be stored in the refrigerator because of its high oil content.

Pecans: a golden-brown, buttery and rich nut. Good in savory as well as sweet dishes; especially good in salads.

Pine: also called pignoli; small, cream-colored kernels obtained from the cones of different varieties of pine trees.

Pistachios: pale-green, delicately flavored nut inside a hard, off-white shell. To peel, soak shelled nuts in boiling water for about 5 minutes; drain, then pat dry with paper towels. Rub skins with cloth to peel.

OIL:

Hazelnut: a mono-unsaturated oil, made in France, extracted from crushed hazelnuts.

Macadamia: a mono-unsaturated oil extracted from macadamia nuts.

Olive: a mono-unsaturated oil, made from the pressing of tree-ripened olives; especially good for everyday cooking and in salad dressings. Extra Light or Light Olive Oil describes the mild flavor of the oil and has nothing to do with fat levels.

Peanut: pressed from ground peanuts; good for stir-frying because of its high smoke point.

Sesame: also called Dark Sesame Oil, it is used throughout Southeast Asia; made from roasted, crushed white sesame seeds and used as a flavoring rather than a cooking medium.

Vegetable: any of a number of oils having a plant rather than an animal source.

ONION FLAKES: packaged chopped and dehydrated white onion pieces; a garnish more than an ingredient.

OYSTER SAUCE: Asian in origin; a concentrated dark-brown sauce made from oysters, brine and soy sauce, and thickened with starches.

PANCETTA: an Italian salt-cured pork roll, usually cut from the belly; used diced in many dishes to add flavor. Substitute bacon.

PAPAYA: also known as pawpaw or papaw; large, pear-shaped, red-orange tropical fruit. Sometime used unripe (green) in cooking.

PAPRIKA: ground, dried red bell pepper (capsicum), available sweet or hot.

PASTA SAUCE, BOTTLED: a prepared tomato-based sauce (sometimes called ragu or sugo on the label) sold in supermarkets.

Cannellini beans

Dried chili flakes

Fresh red serrano chili

Candied ginger

Fresh ginger

Pickled pink ginger

Chinese dried mushrooms

Pancetta

Pastrami

Papaya

V-slicer

Savarin

PASTRAMI: a highly seasoned, cured and smoked beef, usually cut from the round; ready to eat when purchased.

PEARL BARLEY: barley which has had its outer husk (bran) removed, and then steamed and polished before being used in cooking.

PITA: also known as pitta, Lebanese bread or pocket bread; a Middle Eastern, wheat-flour bread, usually sold pre-packaged in large, flat pieces easily separated into two paper-thin rounds. Comes in smaller, thicker pieces commonly called Pocket Pita.

PLUM SAUCE: a thick, sweet and sour, prepared dipping sauce made from plums, vinegar, sugar, chilies and spices.

PROSCIUTTO: salted-cured, air-dried (unsmoked) pressed ham; usually sold in paper-thin slices, ready to eat.

REDCURRANT JELLY: a preserve made from redcurrants used as glaze for desserts or as a sauce ingredient.

RICE:

Arborio: small, round grain, especially able to absorb a great deal of liquid, as in a risotto.

Calrose: a medium-grain rice that is extremely versatile; can substitute for short- or long-grain rice if necessary.

Long-grain: elongated grain, remains separate when cooked; Asia's choice for steaming.

SAFFRON: stigma of a member of the crocus family, available in strands or ground form; imparts a yellow-orange color to food once infused. Quality varies greatly; the best is the most expensive food in the world. Should be stored in the freezer.

SAMBAL OELEK: (also ulek or olek) Indonesian in origin; a salty paste made from ground chilies, sugar and spices.

SAVARIN PAN: a heatproof ring mold named after the baba-like, rum-soaked, rich yeast cake for which it was designed; its use has been extended to include uncooked recipes requiring ring molds, such as a jelly mold.

SEEDS:

Black Onion: also kalonji or nigella.

Mustard, Black: also brown mustard seeds.

Mustard, Yellow: also white mustard seeds.

SEMOLINA: made from durum wheat milled into granules of various sizes and textures; used as a cereal and in desserts.

SOY SAUCE: made from fermented soy beans. Several different types are available in supermarkets and Asian food stores, among them salt-reduced, light, sweet and salty.

SUGAR: the recipes in this book used granulated table sugar, also known as crystal sugar, unless otherwise specified.

Brown: a soft, fine granulated sugar containing molasses to give it its characteristic color.

Superfine: also known as caster or finely granulated table sugar.

SUMAC: a purple-red astringent spice ground from berries growing on shrubs that flourish wild around the Mediterranean. (DO NOT confuse with the common name for Poisin Ivy.) Available from Middle Eastern stores; substitute tamarind concentrate, if unavailable.

TACO SEASONING MIX: a packaged Mexican seasoning mix made from oregano, cumin, chilies and various other spices.

TAHINI: a rich, buttery paste made from crushed sesame seeds.

TAMARIND CONCENTRATE: a thick, purple-black, ready-to-use, sweet-sour paste extracted from the pulp of pods from tamarind trees; use as is, with no soaking, stirred into casseroles and stews.

TAMARIND PULP: the dehydrated meat of the tamarind tree's pods; reconstitute by soaking in a small amount of hot water then pressing through a sieve back into the soaking water. Use the liquid and discard the pulp.

TOMATO:

Paste: a concentrated tomato puree used to flavor soups, stews, sauces and casseroles.

Puree: canned pureed tomatoes (not a concentrate). Use fresh, peeled, pureed tomatoes as a substitute.

Sun-dried: dehydrated tomatoes. The recipes in this book use sun-dried tomatoes packaged in oil unless otherwise specified.

TURMERIC: a member of the ginger family; its root is dried and ground, resulting in the rich yellow powder that gives many Indian dishes their characteristic color. It is intensely pungent in taste but not hot.

V-SLICER: The German company Börner's tradename for an efficient kitchen tool having three different blades to slice, dice and shred vegetables and fruits. Caution is advised when hand-operating this extremely sharp instrument; a mandolin, the generic Italian slicer, or the various cutting discs of a food processor, can be substituted.

VINEGAR:

Balsamic: authentic only from the province of Modena, Italy; made from a regional wine of white Trebbiano grapes specially processed then aged in antique wooden casks to give the exquisitely piquant flavor.

Cider: made from fermented apples.

Malt: made from fermented malt and beech shavings.

Red wine: based on fermented red wine.

Rice: made from fermented rice, colorless and flavored with sugar and salt.

White wine: made from fermented white wine.

WASABI: a Japanese green horseradish paste; sharp and biting so a little goes a very long way.

WATER CHESTNUTS: resembling a chestnut, hence its English name; a small, brown tuber peeled to reveal its crisp, white, nutty-tasting flesh. The crunchy texture is best experienced fresh, however, canned water chestnuts are more easily obtained and can be kept about a month, once opened, under refrigeration.

WATERCRESS: small, crisp, deep-green, rounded leaves having a slightly bitter, peppery flavor. Good in mixed salads, soups and sandwiches.

YOGURT: unflavored, full-fat cow's milk yogurt has been used in these recipes unless otherwise specified. Besides being eaten on its own, yogurt is used in cooking to tenderize and thicken, and is also an ingredient in sauces, dressings and desserts.

ZUCCHINI: also known as courgettes.

124

Index

Make your own stock

These stock recipes can be made up to 4 days ahead and stored, covered, in the refrigerator. Be sure to remove any fat from the surface after the cooled stock has been refrigerated overnight. If it is to be kept longer, it is best to freeze it in smaller quantities. Stock is also available in cans or aseptic containers. Stock base or bouillon cubes can be used. As a guide, 1 teaspoon of stock base or 1 small crumbled bouillon cube mixed with 1 cup (250ml) water will give a fairly strong stock. You should be aware of the salt and fat content of bouillon cubes, stock base and prepared stocks.

Fish Stock
3lb fish bones
3 quarts water
1 medium onion, chopped
2 stalks celery, chopped
2 bay leaves
**1 teaspoon black
  peppercorns**
Combine all ingredients in large pan; simmer, uncovered, 20 minutes; strain.

Chicken Stock
4lb chicken bones
2 medium onions, chopped
2 stalks celery, chopped
2 medium carrots, chopped
3 bay leaves
**2 teaspoons black
  peppercorns**
5 quarts water
Combine all ingredients in large pan; simmer, uncovered, 2 hours; strain.

Beef Stock
4lb meaty beef bones
2 medium onions
2 stalks celery, chopped
2 medium carrots, chopped
3 bay leaves
**2 teaspoons black
  peppercorns**
5 quarts water
3 quarts water, extra
Place bones and unpeeled chopped onions in baking dish. Bake in hot oven about 1 hour or until bones and onions are well browned. Transfer bones and onions to large pan; add celery, carrots, bay leaves, peppercorns and the water. Simmer, uncovered, 3 hours. Add the extra water; simmer, uncovered, further 1 hour; strain.

Vegetable Stock
2 large carrots, chopped
2 large parsnips, chopped
4 medium onions, chopped
12 stalks celery, chopped
4 bay leaves
**2 teaspoons black
  peppercorns**
6 quarts water
Combine all ingredients in large pan; simmer, uncovered, 1½ hours; strain.

***All stock recipes make
about (10 cups).***

Nutritional Information

USDA Nutritional Values

Nutritional values are for 1 cup peeled and trimmed raw vegetables

Vegetables	Calories	Carbohydrates (g)	Potassium (mg)	Fiber (g)	Folate (g)	Vitamin A (g)	Vitamin C (g)
Artichoke, globe (1 med)	109	13	473	7	87	237	15
Artichoke, Jerusalem	117	26	643	2	20	30	6
Arugula	5	1	74	0	20	474	3
Asparagus	23	5	273	2	128	583	13
Avocado	407	16	1458	11	151	1408	18
Beans, shelled	661	120	2877	29	861	33	0
Beans, green	34	8	230	4	40	735	18
Beets	58	13	442	4	148	52	7
Belgian Endive	9	2	79	2	35	512	2
Bell Peppers, green	40	10	264	3	33	942	133
Bell Peppers, red	40	9.6	263.7	3	32.8	8492	283
Broccoli	25	5	286	3	62	1357	82
Brussels Sprouts	38	8	342	3	54	777	75
Cabbage	22	5	219	2	38	118	29
Carrot	50	12	375	4	15	33,000	11
Cauliflower	25	5	303	3	57	19	46
Celery	19	4	344	2	34	161	8
Celery Root	65	14	468	3	12	0	12
Chayotes	25	6	165	2	123	74	10
Corn	132	29	416	4	70	433	10
Cucumber	13	1	75	1	7	112	3
Eggplant	21	5	178	2	16	69	2
Fennel	27	6	360	3	23	117	10
Jicama	50	11	195	6	16	27	26
Kohlrabi	36	8	473	5	22	49	84
Lettuce, iceberg	7	1	87	1	31	182	2
Lettuce, romaine	8	1	162	1	76	1456	13
Mushrooms	18	3	259	1	15	0	3
Okra	33	8	303	3	88	660	21
Onion	61	14	251	3	30	0	10
Parsnips	100	24	499	7	89	0	23
Peas, green	117	21	354	7	94	928	58
Peas, sugar/ snap/ snow	26	5	126	2	26	91	38
Potato	120	26	814	2	20	0	30
Pumpkin	30	8	394	1	19	1856	10
Radicchio	18	2	121	.3	24	11	3
Radish	23	4	269	2	31	9	26
Rutabaga	50	11	472	4	29	812	35
Spinach	7	1	167	1	58	2015	8
Squash, pattipan	56	14.5	486	2	23	476	15
Sweet Potato	140	32	271	4	18	26,684	30
Swiss Chard	7	1	136	.5	5	1188	11
Tomato	38	8	400	2	27	1121	34
Turnip	35	8	240	2	19	0	27
Zucchini	17	4	308	1	27	422	11

Can't boil an egg?

...Then bake it.

Sweet Potato Leek and Sage Frittata (*Healthy Eating Vegetarian*, page 28)